I0165810

LOVE

The Sum and Substance of Our Eternal Reality

ILLUMINATING ENCOUNTERS WITH

MASTER TEACHER

ENDEAVOR ACADEMY
Certum Est Quia Impossibile Est

©2011 Endeavor Academy
Love: *The Sum and Substance of Our Eternal Reality*
Illuminating Encounters with Master Teacher

International Standard Book Number (ISBN-10): 1-890648-04-3
(ISBN-13): 978-1-890648-04-6

Library of Congress Control Number: 2011922371

Published By:
Endeavor Academy
501 East Adams Street, Wisconsin Dells, WI 53965, USA
Phone: +1 608-253-1447
www.themasterteacher.tv
Email: publishing@endeavoracademy.com

Contents

A new commandment I give unto you,
That ye love one another; as I have loved you,
that ye also love one another.
By this shall all men know that ye are my
disciples, if ye have love one to another.

-Matthew 22:37-40

Be My Valentine

L ife on earth is a compromise, a negotiation, an attempt to establish equanimity, reach an agreement where there is none. The latest form of love is the pre-nuptial agreement, drawn up by a lawyer, whereby everybody can still hang on to all their things, but they share some. What kind of relationship would you call it?

(From the audience) "A transaction?"

Yes. A transaction in a search for a particular result.

I want to look at Valentine's Day. So this will be a talk about love. In the last couple of days, I have heard a lot of expressions about what love is, what it isn't, and what it ought to be, and what it seems to be ranging all the way from "God is love" to "Love is a French Poodle." Both of which, incidentally, are true but limiting, in a sense, since God is undefinable and the poodle could only be defined in some sort of non-encompassing rationale as to a comparison of canus domesticus. "What was that? What did he say?"

We must finally love objectively: I love you for your ankles. I love your nose. I love your hair. I love your boobs. I love you for your intellect. I love you for your artistic achievements. I love you for the way you make me feel. I love you for your new boat. I love you because we go to the same church. I love you because you're black or blue or green. I love you because we share a lot of dislikes. I love you because somehow we are going to work through the dilemma of earth in our quest, and together we can find the answers. I love you because my father told me I had to. I love you in defiance of my culture. I love you for all the little things that we share together. I love you despite some particular idiosyncrasies you have, but I'll attempt to change them or just have to go along with them. Amazing, isn't it?

What the heck is love? One thing I'll tell you for sure, it's not a form of exchange. And if you start with that premise, it'll help you a lot. I've heard it said, and well-defined indeed, that love is finally giving. So perhaps before we define love, we should define giving. How many kinds of giving are there? There's the kind of giving I know in exchange, where someone who loves money pulls out a gun and says to you, "Give me your money or I will take your life." And you give him your money. And certainly you're giving it to him. There's the kind of giving that says, "We are required to give to Aunt Tilly a Christmas present in hopes that she will remember us in her will or exchange with us or give us a gift," or "What did she give us last year?" or "We didn't spend enough," or "We're not going to give her anything; she didn't give us anything." There's apparently a nice sort of giving where you, in the goodness of your heart, give something of high value to you — and then you are just a little disappointed when it's not properly appreciated or when the gift you receive in return does not seem commensurate with the value that you have placed on what you've given away. Then there's another level of giving where you give in absolute sacrifice.

You take your life and put it on the altar of mankind and bathe the leper's wounds. You don't attempt to heal the incredible ache and sores that are in your own heart.

The kind of giving that we speak of that's associated and is in fact love, as defined within the nomenclatures we are expressing, is the giving with the absolute recognition of no need for recompense, where the mere idea that something would be returned for the extension of what you have given as a gift would be outside the framework of your consciousness. Indeed, as you transcend your limited identities, you will see that through the extension of you in gift, you receive the love that is a part of what you are.

One of the more difficult things to express to someone on the path is the idea of being a good receiver. You cannot be a good giver if you are not a good receiver. Feeling worthy enough finally to accept any gift that could be offered to you in love is part of the process that you're going through to discover who you really are.

Coming to realize that anything that is not forever cannot be given away is difficult. We are coming to understand, finally, that what we mean by love is creation. Love is only the extension, or projection, of what you think you are. How many times have you said in giving, "This will be a perfect gift for Uncle John. It looks like him." You have placed him in a particular category. You have identified him. Amazing!

The only thing that you can finally, absolutely, totally give away and still have is an idea. An idea is the only thing that the more you give it away, the more you have of it. But remember this, finally you can only be an idea about yourself. And the only thing you can possibly present to someone else as a gift is what you think you are or what you think they are, which is really exactly the same thing.

For what you think they are is only a reflection of what you think you are, isn't it? How much do you really, then, love the recipient of the gift that you are presenting them with? A lot of identities, because of insecurities, are able to love as long as they can keep something at a distance. We can then set up idols that are outside of us and endow them with characteristics or ideas that we admire. They'll fail us eventually, but that's all right. We can establish some other new fresh ones, then, that we can love. And finally reject.

I've heard it said, "I don't know what love is, but I know when I'm in it." Is love, then, an experience? Well, that's getting closer, isn't it? Yes, love is an experience. Creation is an experience. Creation, finally, is your gift from the Essence, from God, and your ability to be a good receiver. The only requirement that has ever been placed on you on this earth is to be able to receive in totalness your own heritage, or the gift of freedom and love that are yours.

"Oh, I know you love me a lot, but how much do you really love me? Will you be my Valentine?" "What do I have to do to be your Valentine? What are the requirements? How much exchange do I have to do?" The idea that in love absolutely nothing is asked in return is extremely difficult to come to in a dualistic consciousness because everything on earth is fundamentally, because of the illusion, based on reciprocity. You think in a sequential manner. You base everything you hope to obtain on what you have previously obtained. And then, it turns to dust. Then you look for something else. Then that goes away. And then you look for something else. You just keep looking. People walk around the earth and say, "All I want is just a little love. All I want is just a little recognition. All I want is just someone to share my life." Is that loneliness real? You bet it's real. When you find that love, is that love real? Holy mackerel, is it real! Why wouldn't it be real, Son of God?

Do you think that the essence of the feelings that you have inside you aren't real? Of course they're real.

Love is love. There isn't anyone in this room that somewhere in this consciousness hasn't felt love so intensely, they didn't know what to do. Have you ever been so much in love, you couldn't stand it? You didn't even want to be close to the object of your adoration. You wanted to just stand back and savor this incredible, ecstatic annihilation that was occurring to your system. You creep out at night so that you can walk by the house and look up at the light. That's a pitiful kind of love. Inevitably your hopes were dashed in some manner. You got up close and discovered that whatever you thought about her was not up to what you expected it to be. But the nature of that need is Godly. Of course. What else would it be?

Love, finally, in a very high form of love on earth, is expectation. There can be no final joy in fulfillment on earth. I am sure most of you are aware of that, because there is in you an innate dissatisfaction because of the need to complete your search or to find the truth of you. So love is sort of like the search for the other half of you, isn't it? There's only half of you. You keep looking for that other half, not knowing that that other half is in you. Will you be my Valentine? I expect you to be my Valentine absolutely and completely. "Well, I'm willing to be your Valentine up to a point."

That's what you say to God, isn't it? If God said to you, "Will you be my Valentine?" You would say, "Sure. What are your requirements?" He says, "Well, one of the requirements, you've got to be happy all the time. You've got to be joyous. You've got to be in ecstasy. You have to extend from you love and see only beauty. Can you do that?" And you say, "Well, who's asking me? How do I know you're really God? How do I know you can really give me those things?" God doesn't even hear you when you ask

11

for something, does He? He already knows that you have everything. It's astonishing. "I can't give you anything but love, baby. That's the only thing I've plenty of, baby." It's amazing. It's a high truth. "Yeah, but do you really love me or are you just saying that?" Amazing, isn't it? That's the kind of love that will bring about your awakening. That's the kind of love all of you have found yourself in the middle of, only to have your ideas dashed to the ground because it didn't turn out to be the way you wanted it to be.

Sometimes it's difficult to understand that absolutely nothing on earth is finally going to turn out to be the way you want it to be, except death. And in the process of accepting death, you have limited yourself to the idea of pain, murder, greed and all the things that go with it on earth. "I want you to be my Valentine, but I don't want him down the street to know about it, and I don't want him to be my Valentine, just you." How early, as children, we are taught to subtract, aren't we? As part of our survival course, we are taught to distinguish and discriminate. When I was a boy we had hate Valentines. They came on little sheets, and they said awful, awful things. People sent them anonymously to other people. They'd say, "I hate you." Now the people we hate, we just don't bother to do anything. We hate them by subtracting them from our lives, from our ideas.

The problem finally, then, is being a good receiver, being able to say, "Okay, I'll take it." Because if I were to give you everything that you could ever ask for on this earth, it would never satisfy you. You know perfectly well it wouldn't, and that's why you're here. You have reached a stage in the maturation of your consciousnesses where you've looked down the line and seen that you're going to die. You've seen death, haven't you? You see that everything here dies. Wow!

"Well, if it's true that you have to give everything away, as Jesus teaches in *A Course In Miracles*, in order to keep it, what's going to happen to me if I believe that and I take all my stuff and give it away?" That's a good question. "That's easy for you to say. You tell me just to extend my love and give it away, but after all, I'm here on the earth. I have to eat. I have to have a house. I have to have a car. I have to subsist. I'm entitled to some things. I want to be able to send out Valentines, have people love me in return for my love. I have to do that, don't I?"

Coming to know the truth of you is a transformative process that has nothing to do with what you finally do in action on earth.

A motivation to do nothing will end up exactly in the same stew as a motivation to go out and attempt to do everything. There is no difference in it. You are on this earth and have constructed this earth because of a limited identification of selfness. As soon as you discover who you really are, the earth will no longer be here. Does that have anything to do with love? Yeah, it has everything to do with love. Because as long as you discriminate in your mind what constitutes beauty and love and desirability to you, you are rejecting other aspects or ideas that you have as less Godly or less true or less lovable. Because you reject these things from your consciousness, they do not disappear. They stay with you. And it is these things that you fear and defend yourself against.

If love is real, and I assure you that it is; if God is a fact, and I assure you that it is; if truth does not require your opinion about it to be true; and I assure you that it is, there could never be any such thing as evil or hate or lack or annihilation or divisiveness or manipulation or needs to identify or needs to perpetuate or needs to defend. "Are you saying, then, that love is only non-active? Is love agape?

Is love nothing but spirit? Is love something that I simply take myself up to some sort of mountain top and dwell in a kind of samadhi, sort of an ethereal neverland?" On the contrary, love is, love is — Amo. Love is totally active, with no objectivity. How do you express something like that? Love is the turmoil of consciousness in the act of being fulfilled. Love is the recognition of the apartness, of the loneliness, of the incredible longing, of the need fulfilling itself. Of course. Is it active? It's totally active! Do you think God's love for you is not finally a state of action? Of course, but not action in the idea of reciprocity, but action in the truth of Itself recognizing Itself. Is my love for you active? You bet your boots it's active. It's what? It's an extension of me. What is creation finally if it's not an identification of beauty, stemming from recognition of beauty of Self, or Source. Wow! What is it that we share together when we paint Valentines or listen to the music? We actively participate in the energies or the rays or the fabrics of consciousness. I'll say we do.

I've seen a lot of definitions of love as being objectively active, where the word love has the same connotation as fornicate, like, "Let me love you tonight. The heck with tomorrow." That's very active. And from that aspect, of course, amo requires an object, doesn't it? Then, again, I've seen it expressed in a very wishy-washy fashion, as we said before, where somebody just sits. It's a state of, "Don't come too close to me. I'm in a state of love. I love only Jesus, and the heck with everybody else." It's an astonishing idea. You want to see real objective love? Look at some exoteric Christianity sometime. "I love my guru, and I'll be unfaithful to him if I come to you." That's a strange idea. You listen to me carefully in regard to love and its objects.

Love is not finally beauty, although I've heard it defined as such. Beauty requires perception. Love requires no perception at all. As a matter of fact, with perception there cannot be true love because if there are degrees of comparison, there is an element of less-than-love involved, and God is never less-than. There is no second to love. I cannot choose to love something and reject something else. That's not love; that's hate. That's tough, isn't it?

You walk up to somebody on the street, and you say, "I love you." What's he going to say to you? "Well, what are you, some sort of nut? What do you want? Here's a dollar. Go get a cup of coffee. Why are you saying that to me? What do you mean, you love me?" Wow! I looked today at the earth, and saw the desperate attempts that the karma identifications, the personas, go through in attempts to communicate with each other. They are unaware of the absolute futility of it. They are unaware, then, that in truth the object — and this would hold with love — of their adoration, literally does not exist except in their own consciousness of it, and they have endowed it with characteristics that they will subsequently deny and reject. Brother Jesus in the *Course In Miracles* expresses it in this manner: He says you literally cannot see your brother, who is standing right next to you; and if you could for just one moment see him, you would see immediately that you share a brotherhood or a union in Christ and would be home together in your love. All you see finally is a facsimile of your own consciousness, of your own memories. You desperately want to love what's outside of you, but since you have literally, because of your association of limitation or guilt, projected the image out from you because you hated it and rejected it, you inevitably cannot accept the love of your own projections. Of course not. How could you? At best you can commiserate with them about death.

Sometimes, the path to find what we're talking about seems sort of rigorous and difficult. We read statements in the *Course*, and I teach in truth that you are afraid of the truth of you. If love attempts to come close to you in any true regard, you reject it and fend it off from you. What do you think love is if it's finally not Christ — if love is not finally man-God? You don't want anything to do with man-God. He would force you to relinquish the limited selfness of you. You're very much frightened of doing that. "Let's compromise together, and I'll overlook what I think you are, partially, and you overlook what you think I am, and maybe we can stay together until death do us part." And I stand in front of you and I say there's no such thing as apartness. You are never alone and literally cannot be alone. In the process of discovering that, you can have an awful lot of lonely moments, because if you didn't feel lonely, how would you ever know that there is such a thing as non-loneliness totally? The same thing could then be said about any experiences that you have ever had in all of your memory banks.

Everything that has ever occurred to you has indeed brought you to this point in time and space, where you are at this moment, hasn't it? Is there somewhere else that you would choose to be rather than here? Is there something better out there that you can love more than you love what you're with now? What is it you're looking for? What is it that you hope to find? You listen to me: You can't find it here; it's not here. There is no love on earth. Finally, when you come to experience in its totalness the feeling of the union that comes about through your transformative process, you will see immediately the falsity of the earth, and the unreality of everything that's around you.

I don't love you despite the things that I think about you. I love you because I know who you are. I don't love you because of qualities that I have given you, comparisons that I have made with you in regard to other personas that are apparently outside of you in this confusion. You are incomparable. Could the Son of God be compared with anything? What would you compare Him with but His Father, of which He is the same? It isn't that you think too much of yourself, finally; it's that you don't think enough of yourself. You limit yourself, don't you? You limit your capacity to love, through inability to accept the idea that contained in you is all of the essence of the consciousness in the universe.

Couldn't the universe love itself totally? What else does it do? Wow. Just look at what love really is. Because love apparently in the illusion of separateness appears to attempt to sustain itself, which indeed it does, does not make it less lovable. Does not God sustain Himself through you? I say to you in truth that there are finally no degrees in Godliness; that the state of beingness, the dharma, God's will is the unity and the singularity; that there is as much Godliness in this pencil as there is in anything in the universe. The universe is not the sum of its parts. Nor is my love for you the sum of adding up the various qualities that you have in order to arrive at the conclusion that you are desirable to me.

How nice it would be if you could finally figure out on the earth that everything would either be totally desirable to you or not desirable in any regard. You would then have eliminated all need to judge anything and would only love. Wow! We then finally give to each other the only Valentine that can ever really be given, and that's ourselves. As long as I hang on to any portion of my Valentine, I cannot love you completely, can I? So I give you love, and I ask nothing in return because there's nothing that you could give me in return, because it's only through the giving of my love to you that I may keep it and be loved.

How could I love if I just sat, separate from something, and allowed something to be outside of me? Indeed, love is active and it is creation. When you come to your final truth, Son of God, you will discover that you are a creator. As I stand before you now, I am actually creating you, am I not? Do you not see that it is your conception that is bringing about your perception? Are you, then, creating something hateful? Are you making something that you don't like, that you want to get rid of? Strange. Jesus in the *Course* says nicely, protect anything that you value by giving it away. Wow! "Well, I tried that, and it didn't work. I went out and I gave a lot of things away. I wasn't appreciated for it. The world's simply no good, and there's nothing I can do about it, so I'll get along the best I can."

The process, finally, of totally giving, or giving of self, is a process of surrender or subtraction — or death is a nice word for it. I am bringing about in you a death process, and you'll still be here after its completion. Isn't that astonishing? Boy, that's a fun idea. There is no death, brother. If there were such a thing as death, how could there be love? Would you simply love something then until it dies? Then find something else to love, and struggle in turmoil. Wow.

Where do you find unity then? Where do you find this truth? In you. The universe finally is only your idea about it. How much do you finally love? What did you reject today as not desirable? How much did you protect yourself today from the projections, from your illusions? The quality of mercy is not strained. That's very nice. Sounds familiar. It's here all the time. Are you, then, a good receiver of the gifts? Be my Valentine. "I'm not going to give you a Valentine this year. I gave you one last year, and you didn't give me one back, and I'll always remember that." All of your grievances, everything that you're holding on to in the past tense; none of it is real. None of it!

For the first time, and I don't mean to think of time as sequential, but in this particular fabric or in this moment, we are attempting to teach the "illusion" (and perhaps that's a word we'll use in this regard). The Atonement or the changing of the mind or the resurrection is totally subjective, and depends absolutely on you to bring it about, and there's nothing outside of you that'll cause it. That's a very difficult idea for you, isn't it? The idea that you are responsible, finally, in your state of consciousness for bringing about peace and glory and heaven and the subtraction of pain, is very difficult for you. But you stop and think just for a moment. If you're in a state of consciousness — and I assure you you are because you say you are — I believe that you think you're you, but you can't tell me who you are, it is going to become more simple for you to accept the idea of maturation, that you are awakening from a dream, that you are coming back to an original origin. There's absolutely nothing new about this idea. It's as old as man and always occurs in revelation.

I'm going to express this to you: Any attempts I make to teach you what occurred to me in revelation are forms of corruption. I say to you that there are quotes in *A Course In Miracles* that are virtually identical to the great Pagan mystic Plotinus, neo-Platonism, or the Christian mystic Meister Eckhart, or more directly Meher Baba — Meher Baba has some quotes in *A Course In Miracles* — or me. It should finally begin to occur to you, on a direct intercession of consciousness that has occurred through scribeship from a different level of consciousness contained in *A Course In Miracles*, that there's one heck of a lot more to you than you have allowed up to this point. For goodness sake. That's what we're bringing about here. It's kind of difficult for you to understand that the only requirement there is, is that you come to your truth. There are no other requirements. Wake up! Wake up! Your creations await you. The tear in the fabric has been repaired. You're dreaming. This is all over.

It is difficult to feel love when you're being attacked by someone, isn't it? I just looked at the dilemma of consciousness where people who want to love are in villages where it seems like they're being constantly attacked and misunderstood. It requires a certain endeavor or determination. Faith maybe is the word. Trust. Make the commitment to Eternal Life or to the idea that there is no death. It is impossible for you to fail, so you be of good cheer.

Do you know something? As you get further and further along on this path, rejection won't bother you in the slightest. That's tough. It's very difficult to teach an initiate this, particularly when they get to a point where they're very sensitive, and they really want to love and they can't understand why they're rejected and why there's so much greed and corruption on earth. For me to say to them, "That's because that's the way that the world is", is difficult. They keep thinking that there must be something outside of themselves that will finally commiserate in totalness with the conclusion they have temporarily arrived at about themselves.

Finally, when you wake up, you will discover that you are absolutely, totally indifferent to what anybody on earth says. Why? Because you know it's not real. The intensity with which the identifications protect themselves is insane. Of course. I'm going to tell you something though. Once you discover the truth for yourself, and it doesn't make any difference to you, you will then begin to extend from you the truth of what you are. You discover that you are me. Who do you think is standing up here doing this? What do you think Brother Jesus finally means when He says in the *Course In Miracles* that God only has one Son? No wonder I love you so much. No wonder I give you everything. Why wouldn't I? What would I hold onto? Nobody can give completely as long as they have a feeling of lack in them.

It's impossible for you to love anyone absolutely until you are love yourself. But you've all had your beautiful moments. The moonlight shining on the lake, the bark of a dog in the distance, the wind rustling through the pines, the pungent smell of mustard plant in the meadow; discovering just a tiny wildflower growing out of a crevice in a rock, a big swallowtail in the morning grass, the incredible feeling of lonely nostalgia when an ancient melody plays in your heart. What else would you finally be but divine? Those moments that you feel of completeness and ecstasy and serenity are part of your heritage. They are the real you. So it will be with you; so it is each moment that you allow it to be — not in preparations for tomorrow or next week or next year, a continuation of a limited idea about yourself, rather coming at this moment into what you really are, discovering through your surrender, through your non-defensiveness the invulnerability of the power that is you.

The species man has a covenant that has been fulfilled, and awaits your return to complete Heaven. That's the only requirement. Happy Valentine's Day! How good a receiver are you? How well can you finally see that it's the giving, and not the object. Sometimes it's a nice process when somebody does something thoughtful in their love for you — and I assure you that you're loved — you look very quickly at the thought that went into them doing that and how they went out and bought it, and thought about it, and planned to give it to you, and looked forward with the expectation of you wanting it. That's the beginning of it, isn't it? True receivers are always very humble because they understand that a giver finally gives through love. That's very lovely.

I accept your gift when you give it to me because I recognize you as the Son of God. I see you creating me in your gift to me. And in my acceptance of your love have I extended mine to you. And indeed there is no difference between giving and receiving, or ever could be.

"I give to you as you give to me, true love, true love." How beautiful are the words that come from the mind of man. Where else in the universe would words or ideas come from except from the mind of man? Are you mindful of your divinity today? Did you act as the Son of God today? I'm teaching a review at the end of the day. Run a quick tape of the day in your mind and say, "I didn't get it quite right this time, but hang on, am I forgiven?" And a big voice will say, "Oh, yeah, you're forgiven." Why don't you go out and make some big mistakes? I'll forgive you for those, too. But you remember this: You can't fool me. I am the truth, and I say that you can't fool me. I have no rationale. I will not finally reason with you. What would you hide from me? I know you. When you begin to do that, you'll have a feeling of cleanness about you. It isn't necessary that you go out and make reparations for things that you have done or imagined wrongs. Forgiveness is of the heart. Are you then afraid to go to the altar and reveal what you really think about yourself? Of course you're afraid. That's why you're here.

You take my hand. We'll go together. I'll take you right up there. When we get up to the last spot, I'll give you a shove and push you right through, and your dream will be over and you'll wake up Home. And you'll go, "Oh, I was dreaming." All of you have had intense dreams that seemed so real to you, and then suddenly you awaken and they are very vivid in your mind, "Oh, I was dreaming." That's what will happen to you when you discover the unreality of the earth. It'll be just like that. You'll go, "Oh!" For many of you, that's occurring now. The more you come into that, the more it comes about. I'd like to have some quiet time.

Good morning. This is another day. It's actually two days after Valentine's Day, but Valentine's Day is every day that you allow it to be, isn't it, through your giving of your Valentine. Somebody said that they felt foolish, and that's what we're going to talk about just for a moment here, because when you're in love, you act in a very foolish manner, don't you. There's nothing finally practical about love. The moment that you make love practical, it's like trying to make God practical. There's absolutely nothing practical about God. How could there be? God is totally impractical. Everything that genius finally teaches, or master-recognition teaches, will always be foolish to natural man, and that includes love or the idea of total love. The idea of total love implies abandonment, or the giving up to the one that you adore — the extension of your total self to that so-called object or that so-called image or that perception.

There is no practicality; there's no rationale in God, finally. He's a burning fire within you that needs to be expressed. That's what you do, all day long. You walk around, attempting to express this joy, this incredible abundance that's in you. What is love, then? Well, we've looked at a lot of things that love isn't. Obviously, love is never a form of exchange in any regard, is it? Love is never objective; it cannot be. Love finally is never exclusive, and cannot be. So we have arrived at a lot of ideas about what love is not.

Now, what is love? Let's come a little closer to it. Love, obviously, is an experience. You agree with that. Would you then agree with me that God is an experience? Since we are in a fundamental agreement that God cannot be defined, that truth cannot be circumscribed, that love can only be experienced, shouldn't we then be about experiencing it? At what point have you, in these three days that have passed since the last talk, gone out and been very exclusive in your relationships? Remember that you suffer from a fatal disease called LP. That's Limited Perception. You are going to die because of it. I saw in the paper this morning that one of the Russian leaders is terminally ill. *Everyone* on earth is terminally ill. Did you think that? I mean, everybody on earth is obviously diseased. They have acknowledged, through their limited perception, the incredible, insane idea of termination. So obviously what's going to occur to them? They're going to be terminated. And with that termination will go their idea of love because their idea of love was limiting. And by limiting themselves, they have limited their innate ability to create, which is really all that love is.

Love is finally my total recognition that I'm making you up, and, by gosh, I better love you. To the direct extent I do not love you, I obviously could not love myself. The greatest admonition that a Christ can ever give is, "Love the Lord thy God with all they might and thy neighbor or thy friend or thy brother as thyself." Exoteric Christianity and being-born-again saviors to the contrary, you cannot love Christ without loving your brother, and the idea that you can is absurd. This is the whole basis of what we teach in *A Course In Miracles.* Of course it's much easier to love God from afar. It's easier to love, to respect, to idolize a guru in a white sheet sitting on the top of the mountain peak, and you can go and visit him, but you don't have to totally identify with him. With your brother you must totally identify. That's why until you find the Christ within you or in your brother, you can never find Him.

Is love, then, a search? Oh, yes! Ah. It's a delightful anticipation of fulfillment, isn't it? Sentences like "I am love." are very true. "The Father and I are one." "I am that I am." Of course. When you have experienced that moment — and all of you here have in moments of fulfillment — they are indelible in your consciousness as peak experiences. We teach in truth that when you transcend or change your mind or resurrect or are saved or are enlightened, you will live and extend from you a constant state of ecstasy — but ecstasy not defined as the opposite of pain, but only as truth or love. Did we get that? That's pretty much there. Which is much the same thing as saying, when you reach that state you will accept everything totally.

There's a point I want to make here. I understand very well that in your projections, when you look at something beautiful, you must judge it as more beautiful than something else. This is an inevitable process. Following your transcendence, what you experience is total self-love, or forgiveness of self, or non-guilt, which gives you a parameter by which you judge everything and love it subsequently. For example, if somebody said, "Do you see a poisonous viper as beautiful as a bouquet of roses?" they are speaking from a position where there is an implication that beauty is not finally a single thing. You remember this in consciousness: Everything is perfect unto itself except you. Can you hear that? You're the insane one. Do you think that that rose is not perfect unto itself? Do you think that that snake is not filled with total self love? Of course it is! Is the leaf on the tree not adorable to itself? Does a rock not churn with the molecules of identification of itself as granite?

25

Of course it does! It knows perfectly well who it is, and it is fulfilling itself. You are the fault. You're the one that's schismed. You're the one that doesn't know who he is. Wow! Wow! You got that? Good. No wonder we teach: *To thine own self be true*, you dummies. If you can't figure that out, how could you ever go outside yourself and find it? You can't.

Now, the subtle difference that occurs in consciousness if you allow for hierarchies is this: The rock knows it is a rock, but it does not know that it is you. You may know that you are you and also the rock. For, indeed, if you are not the rock, you are nothing, because there is nothing outside of truth, which is totalness. Do you see? There is only a state of consciousness. There is nothing else. That's why you can only define yourself as "I am I." There is nothing outside of you. You are the rock. You are the plant. You are the sunset. You are the rich brown earth that we will harvest from. What else would you be but those things? And I don't mean that you feel like a tree. I mean that you are a tree. A little difference there. You know, people walk around and they will feel this energy come up into their throats and they'll glance and they'll see a large porker in a pig pen, and say, "Oh, I can feel that big sow rooting around in the mud. I feel just like it." And that's a great truth. Or you'll talk to the trees, and you feel as though they're talking back. And that's a very real thing. After your final transcendence you have no identity as being separate from the pig, so you can't possibly identify your pigness. Ha! Ha! Ha! I wish I could express this. Do you understand? You become the tree and the pig. That's really what love is, isn't it? Those of you who have experienced real union in mating, when you come together, you can't tell the difference in each other. Of course not. You mate! I'm not recommending that you necessarily mate with a pig! Excuse me! See, everybody immediately tries to go out and act within the limited frame of reference. No. No, no. Love does not have to do with what I'm speaking of; love has nothing to do with that. All that is, are attempts to sustain limited consciousness.

Love defined in limitation will always attempt, after self-identification, to perpetuate a degree of consciousness. That's what the survival of the fittest is; that's what cause and effect are, isn't it? When you overcome that, you will see that indeed you are love and nothing but that. That's pretty much our Valentine's Day talk of love. So how do you feel today? Lovable? Is it possible to feel unlovable for a moment and still be in grace? You bet your boots! In fact, feeling unlovable is exactly the same as feeling lovable. Can't teach that. We'll try. At a particular stage of perception, in order to feel lovable you must have a moment of "unlovability". Do you see? I feel totally lovable now, but just a moment ago I didn't feel lovable. When you become totally lovable, you can't distinguish between unlovableness and lovableness. Of course, because you can't judge it. That's how I know that I love you totally. I don't judge you at all. Wow! That's great highs. Get this, and you'll understand what we teach.

I cannot love you because of your qualities. In my own mind in schism, if I allow lovableness to be a quality, there's an obvious insinuation that there is something unlovable, and that's a fallacy. Everything is lovable. Finally, you come to know there are no degrees of love. When you come to know that, you'll remember everything. You'll return to your creative posture. Jesus in *A Course In Miracles*: Your creations await your return. How long have you been gone? Just a second. You were gone and you're back. You're not really gone.

You haven't really left. You haven't really gone anywhere. This is Heaven. Where would you go? Where can you go to find love? "I'll journey across the universe. I'll climb the highest mountain, go to the deepest valley in search of my true love." Everywhere you go, you are. If you stay here, you are everywhere.

I think finally we might say that love, like truth and God and completeness, cannot be described, but simply is. Sort of like when you're in it, you know you're in it. All we really teach finally is eternal love, because everything that is not eternal is not real. That's what we teach. Fear is death. If you believe you can die, you cannot love. You will simply commiserate. We are here to tell you that you cannot die and must finally be total love. That's all.

You listen to me carefully. We're adding another word to what love finally, really is: It's freedom.

All love on earth binds. Because of your limited state of consciousness, you look for protection in relationships of love and bind yourself to that because of fear. So what you really have is love/fear, or love/hate. If you want to measure your degree of love for someone who apparently is outside of yourself, judge the extent to which you release him. To what extent do you hold on to them because you think you can have love rather than be love? The highest truth that I can give to you is that you can have nothing because you are everything. You cannot finally have love because you are love.

If you want a so-called love relationship on earth to be absolutely successful and absolutely perfect and without deviation and without any elements that are untrue, all you need do is give yourself to it totally. Anything that ever could be lacking in what you construe as a love relationship is what you do not bring to that relationship. Period. Does that answer your questions about relationships, dear brother? That's why all love relationships on earth are compromises, aren't they? You don't know yourself, and they don't know themselves, so you get together and don't know yourselves together. How close is love to hate on earth? Right next to it. How close is love to fear on earth? Right next to it. How close is life to death? Right here, brother. Amen. Thank you.

Thou shalt Love the Lord thy God
with all thy heart, and with all thy soul,
and with all thy mind.
This is the first and great commandment.
And the second is like unto it:
Thou shalt love thy neighbor as thyself.
On these two commandments
hang all the law and the prophets.

-Matthew 22:37-40

Love: The Total Sum and Substance of Eternal Reality

Let's begin with some fundamental suppositions. This world seems to be the necessity to demonstrate our own separate realities within the apparent "facts of life" that constitute our containment in this temporal domain. Now, one thing for sure, it is impossible to exclude the "idea of Love" from this earthly condition of space/time we call human existence. So be it. You are apparently in a human body-garb. You are apparently in an association with forms, ideas, contingencies, actions, perpetration of good and evil, definitions of yourself — but always it would seem, somewhere, in the species of man — pertaining to Love.

Everybody has an idea of Love. I'm going to say, "One, two, three," and I want all of you, everyone in this place, to say basically what you are thinking about Love at this moment. A lot of you are going, "Well, Love is letting go of fear." If that's true, why don't you? I'm not concerned about what you are doing in there. I would just like to hear it.

Quick, think of something; nobody will be able to hear you because everybody will be talking at the same time. I don't care what it is.

Love is my grandma... or sleeping in... or my VISA card. Love is whatever — Love is prunes for breakfast. Love is...

See, now you are thinking. Now I'm going to say, "Love is," and I want everybody to say something. LOVE IS...?

In its fundamental form, Love seems to be a utilization of something. As far as we are concerned, we seem to use Love. Yes or no? "Love makes the world go around." Is that true? Wait a minute. You seem to have all of these lovely definitions of Love when I ask you. But as soon as I ask, "Is that true?" you begin to examine it. Isn't that amazing? You begin to examine it! This, of course, is why we're here. We are going to examine Love.

Let's try once more: God is Love. But what do you mean by that? God is Love. Do you mean that Love and God are the same? Okay, Love and God are the same. What is God? All: God Is Love! That's it? I'm not sure that's too instructional for me. I'm not sure that there's not something else involved in that explanation, pertaining to me. It seems to me that if I ask what Love is, this little book, *All About God* (from *A Course In Miracles* Workbook), says God is Light. This says God is Power. This says God is Giving. This says God is the act of totality of the release of my identity.

So, we are faced somewhere, it would appear, with this definition of Love with another word that would be necessary, and it would seem like it would probably be what, experience? Love is an experience. Is there anyone here, I'm just curious, who has never fallen in Love? Raise your hand. Have you ever fallen in Love?

"I think so."

Haven't all of you somewhere, some time, been in love? Of course you've fallen in Love. "Well I think so" — what kind of answer is that? What do you do, examine it, and then lose it immediately? Come on. Everyone who's fallen in Love has lost it on examination? I think we're getting somewhere. We were in Love as long as we didn't examine it? We had to examine it, didn't we? Yes, of course! How would you know it was Love if you didn't examine it? How would you know what Love is if it wasn't something you could hold onto? How would you know Love if you couldn't look at it and judge it, and compare it to what you think you are and need?

What would it have been if you hadn't been able to examine it? It would have been Love!! You don't get it. It would have been Love had you not examined it! When you examined it, it became what? FEAR! Doggone it. Somebody ought to be able to hear this somewhere.

As soon as you examine Love, it becomes fear! As soon as you possess something, which is what the examination of the association of your mind is, it becomes fearful. Why? It is fearful! Why? You feel you are going to lose it! Of course! Do you want to know how fundamental this is? Do you know why you are afraid to Love here? You are afraid you are going to lose it!! Everyone look into your own mind for a second, and you will see that this is absolutely true. The only reason you have not loved totally is you are afraid you are going to lose it. You actually believe that in the process of giving Love you will lose something. That is the nature of your conceptual mind. It believes that if it gives something away called Love, it won't have any left.

That's not what Love is; that's what fear is! Fear is the fear of loss. Fear is possession. Fear is setting terms for what? GOD! God is what? Love!

Love is eternal. Is Love eternal? Is God eternal? So Love and God are eternal. For those of us who appear to be temporal, in time and space, Love would be a utilization of eternity. The fact is that Love is an essence of the creating, extending power of God. Our demonstrations of it in time will be a utilization of the Power. Ooh, I said an awful word. I'd better stay clear of that word. What did I say? Power! Now I am on very dangerous ground. Do you understand that? What are we faced with? You said to me: "God is Love. God is All Power." Are you telling me that Love and Power are the same thing? What an interesting idea. God is the Power of Love! Incredible idea. Yet wholly and eternally true.

Now let's look at your present condition. God is All Power. Power does not oppose. In your mind, in exchange, Power is a definition of conflict or separation in association with your mind. If all Power is of God and you are afraid of Power, because it has been apparently separated from you, you will be afraid of God. Is that so? In that sense, you are afraid of the Power of God. If that is true and God is your Creator and He endowed in you all of His Power, you must be afraid of your own Power!

If you are afraid of your own Power, you will be afraid of your Power of Love. You will literally be afraid of the passion of your association with the divine Love of God, because to you it is a form of opposition. That is, the Power of God will literally strike you dead instead of Love you eternally. This is the Fourth Obstacle to Peace in the divine origination called *A Course In Miracles*, in case you haven't discovered it. You are afraid of Power! Total Power frightens you entirely.

So you are afraid of the total Power of Love. Do you see that? Since you are afraid of it, you retain it. You share it and you limit Power. You might want to say that the world is nothing but an attempt to contain Love. The whole association of the human condition is an attempt to contain and possess the Love of God within its association because of its fear of Love. It is literally afraid of the passion of its own mind in association with the creative purpose with which it is endowed. It is scared to death of its own Love. Wow!

"If I give myself to Love, I won't have anything. I'm afraid to Love because I'll be hurt." Do you realize the magnitude of the human condition? It's afraid to Love totally because it's going to be hurt. If it gives itself away, it's bound to be hurt. It's bound to lose. It'll be misunderstood in its intentions. There will be no reciprocity in regard to its give. It's willing to give up and sacrifice its limited definition of itself, and it's going to be hurt because it gave away Love, which is God. It literally is fearful of its own giving! It has become a judgment of fear. Isn't that so?

Remember that God only gives! Life is only eternal giving. The act of an uncontrollable admission of God is what Love is, and the only thing that little mind of yours is afraid of is loss of control! What you are most afraid of is that Love is uncontrollable. Love is uncontrollable! What a terrible thing to say in this world.

"Oh, I seem to be possessed with uncontrollable Love." If it is uncontrollable, you can't be possessed by it! How can you possess it if it is uncontrollable? All of your attempts to control Love are what fear is! You attempt to control it; you regulate it, you deregulate it, you give it, you take it, you exchange it. But there is one thing that you will not do. You will never become totally uncontrollable. If you did, you would spring into Heaven! All of your efforts to contain God are what is keeping you from seeing that God is Love. It's that simple. They're going to hang me for this, because it doesn't seem to involve all sorts of ethics. It doesn't seem to involve lots of things like "I've got to Love and honor, and I've got to take care of my children." Actually, it involves them totally because they are products of your mind, and in your forgiveness of yourself is their salvation. So don't let them be just forms of possession. That is not what Love is, if God is only Love. Father, into thy hands I commend my spirit (Luke 23:46) is what you do not intend to do. Yet, except in that you do that, you cannot know that you are Love. You are Love!

Here's the problem: Since you are in an act of association in forms of your mind, you require, within your own conceptual self, a demonstration or the need for verification of the Love of God. Otherwise, you would not be here! Somewhere I'm going to have to give you the commandment: Thou shalt love the Lord thy God with all thy heart, and with all thy soul, and with all thy mind. (Matthew 22:37) What are the three things? Heart, mind, spirit — or the act of bringing the heart and the mind together.

Notice that we did not subtract your mind from the process. You can love God very reasonably because He is all there would be. So then I can have the act of dependence on Him. The act of dependence on God in the reasoning process will be what Love is. The act of the dependence on God is what Love is! Now I'm involved immediately with the heart. "I will love Him with all my heart" means "God, in You I trust." The moment that I trust in God completely, He will be completely reasonable to me in my mind. The idea of a whole, loving God is completely reasonable. It doesn't require any definition, except the certainty of the give. That's what the spirit is... "with all my soul." With everything that I am in this association, I will love God.

There is one more thing, which is exactly the same — *...and thy neighbor as thyself.* (Matthew 22:39) It would be impossible for you to love God and not God's creations. If your neighbor is a creation of God, as you are, how could you not love your neighbor? As a matter of fact, this admission of Jesus does not involve the heart and soul and the spirit at all. He says, "Love thy neighbor", which is the same thing. What He says is, the moment you give yourself entirely to your neighbor, you will discover that your neighbor is you! In that, you are loving or giving to yourself in the entirety. You obviously believe that exchange is possible, and that by giving away a part of you, you will actually lose God's Love. What you are holding onto is fear. What you are holding onto, as defined by this world, is not Love; it is fear. You say, "Yes, but I experience it as Love." Yes, you do. Oh my. Just for that moment of gratification within your own mind, you experience what? The Love that is all around you. Ah, but then your need to define and possess it binds you once again to your space/time termination.

Do you see! In your definition of it you retain it, through fear of the loss of it within your own temporal association. In that sense, what you are saying is, "I love my existence — I love death. I love the things that I do." Now we have some conflict going on! This earth is not eternal. It does not extend forever, so it is not Love. Anything that is not Love is not God; therefore, this earth is not Lovely or Godly. If it is not Lovely or Godly, it cannot be anything!

There is the conflict and the message you are providing to the association. That is to say, this is either God's Love totally, or it is what? Nothing! But if it is indeed nothing, then all of your concerns about pain and death and loneliness and fear are totally meaningless because they are not a part of God's Love. If you are afraid to lose

LOVE: ILLUMINATING ENCOUNTERS WITH MASTER TEACHER

it, it is not Love! That doesn't mean you won't go through periods when you think you found it and subsequently lose it. But you can't lose the Love of God. It is impossible. To you, the necessity to defend it is the guarantee of the loss of it, because if there's one thing you are afraid of, it is the entirety of God's Love. To you, Love is a containment. Do you understand that? To you, it is a form of holding on to something until the passion grows so intense — obviously it is rage, because it is an inability to define yourself within your own association. You impose limitations on your own mind, and rage in your inability to find Love. Yet it is only you who has contained it in your own mind and will not allow it to be what it is.

It seems to be an act, doesn't it? Do you sometimes say I love you? Why don't you say I love me? I don't have to say that. I already know that. God is me, and I love God.

I need to say I love you because you appear to be outside of me. This is called forgiveness. I need to release my definition of you in association with myself, and through the auspices or power of Love I will experience God's Love with you. Now, in that sense, it is a utilization in my mind of God's Love. That is what healing is. The utilization of God's Love in my mind, the totality of the Holy Spirit, repairs the image of the separation of myself from my brother.

In this little book [*All About God*] it says God is Light, God is the Mind with which I think. It will say God is Love, but it contains a qualification — it will say: God is the Love in which I forgive. The act of forgiveness is the requirement for Love on earth. There is no possibility — if you are in a possession of associations of a definition of yourself and your brother — that you can Love. It is a containment of the evil possessions of your own mind in a demonstration of your power to usurp the eternal mind of God and suffer the conflicting results of the definition of what is not Love, but is rather hate and murder and death. It gets a little tough, doesn't it? Pure Jesus of Nazareth! So beautifully imperative. So uncompromising. So real.

Maybe I need to say I love you.

Is it possible to say I love you without there being a definition of the manner, means or correspondence by which we Love with God?

Why are you asking me? Why do you ask me if unconditional Love is possible? Obviously to you, unconditional Love is not possible. You are requesting what the condition is for you to Love your brother as yourself. Since Love is unconditional, there are no requirements except the loss of your control. Obviously to you, loss of control is what fear is. But to God — to Jesus, to me, to your awakening mind — what you are experiencing here (the loss of your self-conception) is God's Love! Through not attempting to manipulate or define or associate in your own thoughts, you experience Love — or the miracle of your entrance into the Kingdom of God.

The un-doing of possessed love (which is what hate and fear are) is God's Love at the moment of its un-doing. It would have to be true because Love is everything. If Love is everything, each moment that I don't deny, in the correspondence of my own conceptual self, the totality of my creating power associated with God's Love, I will what? Experience Love!

This may very well result in I love you. Why? You are in a process of coming together from separation. The expression, "I love you", is an expression that I love God! I am in Love. I am in an apparent uncontrollable condition (at the minimum) to the dedication to seek an alternative to this. Brother, it starts with that! It starts with the idea that this cannot be Love. If God is Love, what is this? This cannot be Love.

I understand, as Saint Paul did, that you are going to end with all of the things that Love isn't. Every time you think that Love is something, you are wrong. In First Corinthians, Paul, an awakened mind, attempts to consolidate the Love of Christ in His resurrection with the church that is forming — this church. There are a lot of good admonitions in First Corinthians concerning what Love is, and more directly concerning what you are evolving to as members of the church of Christ — or as members of the entirety. It's nice reading, and I'm going to read it today. Paul goes to great lengths to explain to you that the power of the separate body coming together as a single body will utilize various techniques of the expression of Love. You are asked to be tolerant in the certainty that we are all, as a church, only the single body of Christ. If this is valuable to you, read First Corinthians. Some of us will speak in tongues. Some of us will demonstrate our Love through Light. Some of us may be able to intellectually correspond.

Understand me, as I stand here with you. I have no concern at all about the manner in which you express the new action of your mind in its certainty of self expression regarding your creating power. You will have a tendency because of your separate associations to wish to speak in tongues. Go ahead. So what? You will go beyond this. Use what God has given you (which is everything) to express everything that you are. Love is not a definition of your abilities to express it! That is not to say that the power of your mind in the reorganization of your own association will not become an extension of God creating. Why would it not, if the retention of the momentary (what you call) spatial/temporal association has denied you the totality of access to the Love of God? Who didn't understand me? Christians? If you value it, give it away! If you value it and possess it, it will not be Love; it will be death! The act of giving away is the sharing of God's Love.

I think I'm getting uncontrollable, but instead I discover a new recognition of myself and this world. There's a surety that you won't lose control. We have directed you sufficiently so that you are somewhere now in time aware that you are in a process of returning to Love. It will become very exciting to you because Love is exciting. Love is literally the loss of fear that you thought was necessary in order to be loving. The discovery of this is amazing many of you because Love now has become what? Freedom! You have freed yourself of the possession of the necessity of loss contained in your cause-and-effect relationships. That's why so many of you are laughing. Is that why you are laughing?

In a particular sense, you have freed yourself momentarily from body identification. Let's have some fun. When Paul organizes this in Corinthians, he will organize it first in talking about the church, including "Ladies, leave on your hats." Of course, it is always misunderstood. Ladies, in particular, have to keep their hats on, because female is the potentially contained energy, and if the ladies take off their hats, they will disrupt the association with new space/ time definitions. How very true that is. Here are all these priests up there: "Ladies keep your hats on!" That reduces to "Don't bring your female sexuality into the church — you will disrupt our containment." You are afraid of the power of your potential. You protect it. "You wear a hat so we can protect you and keep you contained within yourself."

And you allow us to do that, because you are the protective agent within your own self that requires this association. Obviously, this is not definable. Just as obviously, those who are fearful of Love will define it. Do you see that? They will talk to you and write letters about your appearance. "The least you could do is hold some decorum. Whatever you do, don't release and trust God. You are liable to lose all of these things. You will not be able to possess along with the rest of us and die with the rest of us."

You are laughing at that. But I assure you that yesterday that was not funny to you; that was a direct attack on your condition. To you, conditional love was a necessity for your own existence. You don't realize the magnitude. Never, until this moment, have you realized the magnitude of the threat of Love to this association. Love is totally threatening to an identity of separation. Just as eternity, extending forever, is the only threat that space/time will ever have. Space/time is your denial of eternity. It is threatened consistently with eternity. So it eliminates itself (which is really absurd if you look at it) and calls it death. That way, it can demonstrate by the loss of its own possession (which it calls love) that it can die. Now, what it calls love (or possession) is connected to loss. Do not underestimate the insanity of the human condition.

Is this really all that Jesus, or any awakened mind, teaches? There is no such thing as loss! All of your control is a demonstration of your authority to die. Shame on you. You will not succeed in doing it. I'm talking to you directly. It is impossible for you to succeed because you cannot escape the Love of God. You are doing everything you can as a human being to define Love as your limitation so that you can suffer loss and sacrifice and kill to honor this lord of death that is going to creep up on you and cause you sickness and loneliness and death. You are insane. You are simply asleep in a dream of separation. This is an absurd place. I'm teaching *A Course In Miracles.* I love *A Course In Miracles* because it's your course to Heaven and you are the miracle. This is all that it says. And this is what you have always denied. What? The Love of God!

The apparent loss of control is only an entering in, momentarily, to a new continuum of association of space/ time, an extension of the single purpose for us being here. You cannot come to God without a momentary loss of control of yourself. I know that you, each moment, will define the new control that you are exercising in order to justify your necessity to come to it. Certainly this is part of your whole mind. All I am telling you is that you cannot escape the Love of God.

You say to me, "I'm not trying to escape it."

Then I say to you, why are you in this world? Why are you here suffering in the body?

And you say, "Well, I have to be."

And I say, no you don't!

Now I'm going to teach you how you can come to know that you are the Love of God through the rejection of the tolerance of your old, long-gone individual association of pain and death that previously totally involved your historic mind. You have been a liar from the very beginning. There is no part of you that is not whole and perfect — this is Paul. Right after he explains Love, he declares that there is only one God. You cannot escape from the fundamental principle of Universal Mind.

So you find yourself in a condition, in a body, individually, experiencing the Love of God with the necessity to contain it as an expression of yourself and die. Astonishing! You need what? A miracle! You need the miracle of Love that is all around you if you are not predetermined to exist in this continuing hallucination of separation. Do you understand? Jesus, in the *Course*, teaches you have one single problem, and that is your apparent separation from God's Love — from Life!

Separation from Love is what fear is. Stop trying to find in your own mind a definition of what Love is, if God is only the totality of your own creation. Many of you are discovering, to your amazement, that there is a God. It will say here reasonably in this little booklet, *All About God and How to Find Him*, that God is my strength in which I trust, God is my vision, there is nothing to fear. It also says God is the Love in which I forgive. But God knows nothing about it. God only Loves. This will say that the auspices of God's Love allow you to use the power of His mind to release the necessity for the defense and condemnation of your brother. Do you see that? God doesn't forgive.

You say, "God is going to forgive me." God doesn't forgive. God Loves! You say, "He forgives." No, He Loves!

God knows not of forgiveness. He only Loves. He has never condemned. And there must be condemnation before forgiveness is necessary. Forgiveness is the great need of this world, but that is because it is a world of illusions. Those who forgive are thus releasing themselves from their own contained illusions, *while those who withhold forgiveness are binding themselves* to their own possessions. *As you condemn only yourself, so do you forgive only yourself.* [From the booklet, *All About God and How to Find Him*, Workbook Lesson 46]

"Well, I will forgive him if he forgives me." Brother, it is going to start with you, because he is a projection of your unforgiving mind.

Asking him to forgive is the same as asking fear to Love. Once more: Asking him to forgive is the same as asking the fear, which is a product of your own mind, to Love. You cannot change the effects of your own mind. He cannot Love because you do not Love. "...and thy neighbor as thyself." That's what this says: "...and thy neighbor *as* thyself." You forgive only yourself.

Listen: *Yet although God does not forgive, His Love is nevertheless the basis of forgiveness* — because His Love is everything! *Fear condemns and Love forgives. Forgiveness thus undoes what fear has produced, returning the mind to the awareness of God. For this reason, forgiveness can truly be called salvation.* As long as you hold pain and fear within your own mind, you cannot enter the Kingdom of Heaven. That's not open to a discussion. That's the fact of the matter. Only in your own mind is the solution of the separation from God. Wow! It is the means by which illusions disappear. Here is the exercise: *God is the Love in which I forgive myself.*

Now we have that God is Love. And we also have that God is all-powerful. And we also have, therefore, that Love is Power. And all Power is given unto you in Heaven and earth. What you are experiencing is the new Power of God that is actually what Love is. Please don't try to define Power and Love separately. If you do, you will contain yourself in the limited power of your capacity to express pain and death — what you would call a facility — that can express the totality of using the limited power of your mind. Why is that so? You are afraid of Power. The only reason you are here is that you are afraid of God. Not only are you afraid of God, but you will say that's one of the things you have to do first: Fear God. That's true because you do fear God. The admission that you fear God allows you to examine the reasons why you fear Him. Until then your condition is hopeless. There is no question that you are afraid of Love, which is what God is.

You can't lose Love, can you? All earthly possessions or special relationships are retentions of sickness and death, and not Love. You are capable of two emotions; one is Love and the other is fear. This earth is fear. This Heaven is Love. There is no comparison between the two. Fear is the denial of Love. You make it so difficult, when it's so simple.

"I don't know what to do." Do nothing! This is an un-doing. "I am no longer able to understand it." Good! I will stop trying to understand it and I'll use this person to experience the Love that he is extending from me to me. Where I previously defined him within our limitation and loved him because he was himself separate, which associated with me (so that I could define myself in the egotistical manner in which I define him), I will now Love him through the release of my necessity to identify him as the only living Son of God. Why? He is the only living Son of God. But certainly not because you've identified him thus.

"Well," you say, "am I the only living Son of God, too?" No, just him. You said, "Too".

He is the only living Son of God. That's called forgiving your brother. It is not a definition of me; it is a certainty of him. I am certain about him because where he was previously a projection of my mind, my new enlightened mind — available to me in its entirety — is using this fabric of Holy Spirit called Unifying Energy Love Association. It is always available to me, and I'm sick and tired of the limitations and restrictions that I paste on this Power of the Will of God when I exercise my will in the limitations of my apparent temporal identity. I am not going to do it any more. Are you ready for this? I don't do it. I am teaching you not to do it. Miracles are all around you. Stop defining yourself as a body in the nothingness of old memory. This is a complete undoing of all of your self-conceived nothingness.

I am telling you: Don't do exchange! Don't express a necessity for exchange of what Love is — this is nothing but eye-for-an-eye, come on! If you do, that will not be Love. It will be fear because your need to exchange Love is what fear is. Got it? Your need to exchange is fearful. How would it not be? The reciprocity, the idea of judgment, everything that you do is a form of fear.

You say, "Well, I know that, but how will anybody here know how much I love God?" They won't.

I'll try Paul here for a minute. I'm actually declaring First Corinthians. "How will anybody know?" They can't know! They are a denial of the Love that you are experiencing. Your need to have them know denies you the totality of your own access to God. Of course! That is what this will say. This is what Love is not. Everybody loves these passages: "Love is not puffed up...it's not this, it's not that...it's not human things and expressions..." In that sense, it is a demonstration of God's Love, not your own. Your own definition is not true. Love is not an exchange. Love is not an idea of holding on to scarcity.

In the King James version, the word that is used is charity, isn't it. The translation in your Bible may read, the greatest of these is Love. In this Bible it reads, the greatest of these is Charity. The closest that the human condition can get to the giving of the Love of God is "charity." Quite literally it is giving to those who have less than you. Do you see that? So the definition of Love is giving, which would be charity — that is, loving thy neighbor as thyself is giving thyself to thy neighbor. Do you understand? Remember that charity is an act. If you give to the poor, the act of giving is what Love is — not the exchange or reciprocity of it. In the act of giving, you enter into the essence of the extension of God, which is only God Mind giving. His giving to you *totally* is what He is and what you are.

The way you know that God gives is by your giving. That is what Love is. Love is *That*. It may appear to be other things in the association. I may use my mind, I may use my heart, I may use my spirit, but Love only gives. How fearful that is to you. How fearful the loss — to actually lose, within your own mind, the associations that possessed you that you were fearful of losing. In that act of losing them, you are very fearful. Why? Love is entering into your association. But it doesn't seem like Love at the moment it enters in; it seems like fear, because everything you do is exactly the opposite of what it is. Your love is fear and your fear is of love.

Paul will say that regardless of what I do, the greatest of these will only be Charity or Love, that everything else doesn't mean anything if it is not loving. Any attempt to define the act of Love will be a reduction thereof. This is the condition that the world suffers from. If I stand now before a congregation and I'm demonstrating a preaching capacity or capacities to heal or suddenly you jump up in spirit and handle snakes and do all the things that you do, that's perfectly all right because these can be demonstrations, as we said before, of the members of your churchhood coming together in the realization of the end of this continuum. But you listen to me: Without Love you will be nothing! Do you get me? Now you are going to move all sorts of mountains, but what the hell does that mean? All it means is the verification of the temporary separation. You are using the power of Love to do that.

Though I speak with the tongues of men and of angels, and have not charity, I am become as sounding brass, or a tinkling cymbal. (I Cor 13:1) That means this: If you reduce the form of your expression of passion, the real gold of happiness and joy that is God will turn to the brass of the narrowness of fearful idolization of the passion of the expression of yourself. All of your definitions of yourself are containments of your passion of creative ability, without exception. You always reduce them somewhere to clashing cymbals. You hear them as breaking glass and things that go with it. Why? You have restrained the reality of your creative mind.

I am become as sounding brass, or a tinkling cymbal. And though I have the gift of prophecy, and understand all mysteries, and all knowledge; and though I have all faith, so that I could remove mountains, and have not love/*charity, I am nothing.* (I Cor 13:2) Listen to me! Not that I am something that does not have Love — but that I am nothing. Except that I am the Love of God, it says I am nothing. Don't be concerned about how you demonstrate it. Moving mountains is nothing. What would that have to do with the real power of God? Why would God move mountains? Where is He going to move them? It is just absurd. You are so limited in your definition of yourself. Wow! Look at this:

And though I bestow all my goods to feed the poor, and though I give my body to be burned (sacrifice), and have not love/charity, it profiteth me nothing. (I Cor 13:3) There is no profit in exchange. The profit is the giving of the totality of the nature of God. Let's see if I can do this for you: If there is a profit of Love, it can be laid up in stores of holy instants, but not by the verification of the utilization of the Love to move mountains. Jesus calls that magic, doesn't He? He says, don't use the power of your mind to move mountains. You are so contained in your little nothingness that you will just keep twisting around and around in your own conceptual associations. You don't want to do that.

Charity suffereth long, and is kind... (I Cor 13:4) It is not concerned at all about its relationship with itself. Am I long-suffering? You bet!

"But you told me you didn't suffer."

I did not! How would I know that I'm real and here if I didn't suffer? I have included my suffering in with what I am. If I include my suffering in with what I am, it would be impossible for me to suffer, because I am what? Love! You mean that Love is suffering? Sure! What the hell is wrong with Love being suffering, if Love is everything? If you want to define Love as limitation of suffering, go ahead. You want to lose it? Go ahead. But why, except in hell, would you want to use the power of your own mind to suffer?

"Well, you told me that suffering is not Love."

No I didn't. I told you that you are Love. If you suffer, you will be Love suffering! There is no God without you, is what I said. Obviously God, your Creator, does not suffer! Obviously you do. Something is fundamentally wrong.

You say, "I am going to have to include my suffering in."

Let me see you do it. The moment that you would include your suffering in, it would disappear. What do you do instead of that? You make your brother suffer! By making your brother suffer, you escape from your own suffering.

Who sees this? Say: I Love You! All: I Love You! Perhaps that's better than Amen!

Do you know why there are no so-called earthlings in temporal existence who continually experience their own creative reality (union with God)? Shall I answer? When they have this experience, they are no longer of this earth! Come on, dummies. This is the experience of God's Love! If you experience God's Love, you are not on earth! Stop looking for Love where it isn't. It's not here!

"How do I explain this experience?"

You can't. As you leave the earth, you might want to scatter a little of your Love around. My prayers are not to the earth; my prayers are to you — you are the ones who are hearing me. I don't pray for the release of sickness, pain and death that is apparently this world. This world is not reparable because it is not real. That has nothing to do with me. I pray for you as you emerge from your own fear to your own Love. Your mind is split but is fast becoming whole. You were trapped between fear and Love. You can't be totally fearful. It is impossible. You might as well be totally loving, because that's what everything is. You will not succeed in being totally fearful, which is what death is, because you can't die. You have heard your call — I'm just your constant reminder. It's time to go home.

Charity suffereth long, and is kind; charity envieth not; love/charity vaunteth not itself, and is not puffed up. (I Cor 13:4) The translation of not puffed up is: "not contained in its own credential identification," puffed up meaning putting all the degrees after your name. It is puffed up in the idea of knowledge that you have gained in the containment of the little kingdom that you rule that falls to dust, and all of your credentials are totally meaningless and this is why you don't want to hear the message. You are so puffed up with your own computerization of Love, that you bind yourself to the correspondence within your own mind. To a mind emerging, this little puffed-up-ness is what makes you laugh. The guy will contain himself and puff himself up and give you all of these egotistical definitions — he's an egomaniac — which is what a human being is. He will give you all of the definitions of himself, which are totally meaningless. I know you are going to call it Love, and I know you are going to say that you must hold onto this in order to Love. As long as you hold onto that, you will be denying and attacking God. There is no in-between.

I know you don't like these sentences, but that's how it is. Planning for the future is an attack on God.

You say, "Oh, you don't mean that."

Yes! I mean exactly that.

You say, "Well, how can I not plan for the future?"

Simply don't plan. Don't hold old, gone-away thoughts in your mind. Obviously that is going to have to come down into some sort of action. But I want to show you that it must start with the uncompromising statement that God is Love, and this is not. Until then, there is no relief. If you allow me to offer you the Kingdom without immediately killing me as one of your old projections, you will begin to experience the Love of God.

Many of you don't understand what happened here. This continuum made the mistake of allowing for the emergence of an association of Love. Now this is going to be broadcast in a moment, and everybody is going to stand up and kill you. I'm confirming Jesus here. Of course they're going to, because you are offering them unconditional Love. The only, greatest threat they could ever have is the passion of your uncontrollable Love for God. It doesn't have anything at all to do with the world. Why? Because the Love of God has nothing to do with your old associations. Know ye not that you must be born again? (John 3:3) If you are born out of this earth, you will spring up into Heaven, and the earth will mean nothing at all to you. Are you sure you have that?

Charity rejoiceth not in iniquity, but rejoiceth in the truth. (I Cor 13:6) Love does not rejoice when somebody gets his own come-uppance. One of the toughest things to do is to not say, "I told you so." One of the toughest things to do is not feel that the rapist deserves to be punished. Why? He deserves to be punished.

Then you say, "Yeah, but what am I going to do with him?"

What do I care what you do with him?

"Doesn't he deserve to be punished?"

Yes, but so do you. If he deserves to be punished, so do you. What are you going to do? Measure the degrees of what is not Love? Isn't the measurement of it what is not Love? Isn't your determination to sin and to believe there are degrees of it a containment of yourself and a denial of God?

To say to you that you will not feel the emotion of the necessity for justice in the association is not true. You must experience it. If you don't at the moment experience it, you would not be human at all. The release or forgiveness is the act of the certainty that you, as an enlightened consciousness, are not of this world. If you will look at it in that regard, you will see that nothing is more vicious and killing and murderous than a female protecting its young. I just want you to see that. I'm not going to give that talk — but the possession is vicious.

Here comes Jesus; here I come, and I say, and He says, I am not concerned about the rapist, because the rapist can only be a thought of your own mind. Now you are going to condemn me, which is the same as killing me. You must kill me by judgment of me. If not, you would have to admit that you are the thought of rape; that all sin is a construction of self-identity. This is Sermon on the Mount.

I cannot offer you the solution because you retain it in separation and want to know why I am talking about rapists. I'm not. I'm talking about your mind, about your own false ideas about yourself. I'm talking about anybody or anything you want to talk about. I'm talking about cancer, I'm talking about heart attacks and loneliness and pain. I'm talking about death, I'm talking about loss.

I am standing here with you now, sharing a moment in time, telling you this place is not real. This is what this is going to say. It is going to say that there isn't any such thing as separation from God. And that is what you have not wanted to hear. But, doggone it, there isn't any such thing as separation from Universal Mind. I know it is the one thing that you don't want to hear, because you are the one thing that hasn't heard it. But it is impossible that you do not know about it, because I am telling you about it.

You are the one that told me God is Love. I agreed. You are the one that told me there is eternal life. I agreed. You are the one that told me, "I am feeling happy and free and ecstatic in the Love of God." All I am doing is agreeing with you!

The only place where I would disagree with you is in the idea of "place." You believe that the containment of yourself is a definition of reality.

Remember, this is what Love is: Beareth all things...

(I Cor 13:7) The moment that you let it come in on you, it will turn to light and be gone. For goodness sake. The only thing that you could possibly crucify is your own self. Stop examining it. You happily bear all things — why wouldn't you? You are all things! What's the difference between bear and bare? All the difference there is. Do I bear it, or do I bare it? If my burden is light, I bare myself. So I'm going to bare myself, because my burdens that I thought were my sins are really nothing — and my burdens will be light. There is an all-ness in this that is obviously not acceptable.

Beareth all things, believeth all things... (I Cor 13:7) You are going to be what you are in your own association. What is that going to have to do with Love? Love believeth all things because it is innocent of judgment or the disbelief in God. God is a belief or a faith in the totality of God. It has nothing to do with the exchange of what you think I am. What you think I am has nothing to do with what I am or what you are. Now I am free to be with God. Why would I want to set up a defense of myself from your accusations? The defense of myself from your accusations — humans — I'm talking about me as the savior, is nothing but the admission of the possibility that you can attack me. It is not true. But just as obviously, you will attack me and insist that I define you in your relationship of what is not Love. Now I am attempting to define Love to you. But it is obviously not acceptable to you. Obviously it is not. Love is the giving away of your own possessed self. This is so uncompromising! Salvation is simply no compromise.

Believeth all things, hopeth all things (everything is possible), *endureth all things. Love/charity never faileth.* (I Cor 13:7-8) Why? It doesn't know failure. God, who is Love, does not know what failure is — unless He could fail Himself. Since God cannot fail Himself, Love cannot fail. Listen to me carefully: Everything else you do in regard to Love will fail because everything you do here is a definition of failure, not of Love, because all definitions of actions of coming from falsity to truth are not what Love is.

Now you are going to say to me, "All of this is going to pass away? And all of the prophecies?"

Yes, of course. So what? God is Love. God is not this.

Charity never faileth: but whether there be prophecies, they shall fail... (I Cor 13:8) Why do prophecies fail? Because the idea of prophecy is the idea of the possibility. Contained within any prognostication is the idea of failure. Somewhere the prophecy would have to fail, because the prophecy of wholeness or Love has already been fulfilled. As you remember the prophecy that you are whole as God created you, you fail in this entirely, and lose the capacity of failure. That's why Love never fails. The prophets, they shall fail. Prophets are going to fail. John the Baptist is going to fail. Herod is going to cut off his head. He proclaimed the coming of the Christ. Christ came and resurrected. What are you doing here? You killed your prophet. You wouldn't even let your prophet come. Even to John: Jesus told John's followers to go tell John in jail that, "I came." You are going to go to jail for me. You are going to say, "He's coming," you are going to do all those things in your prophecy.

I am telling you it is time to let your prophecy fail, not succeed, because letting your prophecy succeed will condemn you to the continuing idea that prophecies can be fulfilled. Did that come around too fast for you? Obviously, God is not a prophecy; He is a reality. You may appear to fail.

Many of you have come to me and have said, "I have done everything I can do, and I can't make them understand. I'm failing." I say: No! It's working!

I saw George Burns in "Oh, God" yesterday. If you haven't seen "Oh, God," be sure and see it. How many have seen "Oh, God?" You forgot about it. Go see it again. There's much expression of the necessity for faith, and there's a lot of lovely stuff. God appears and tells a grocery man that He is God and gives him a message that they should love one another. He tries to convince someone that he has talked to God, and of course, it's impossible. At the end, he says, "God, nobody hears this." And God says, "No, it worked good. It worked perfectly. You can't fail."

Now, being unable to fail is the only thing that is going to finally make you real happy. You won't need a justification for the act of your own mind. It isn't that you succeed; it is that you fail. In your failure to do it is the realization of the non-necessity to accomplish, because you are no longer possessed by your apparent successes. If you are possessed by your successes, you will continue to succeed in denying and attacking God. Wow! Everything is the opposite.

Protect everything you value by the act of giving it away, and you will be eminently successful. You can't fail if you give everything away. How could you; you have nothing to fail. You give everything away, and you will be free! You have only been attacking yourself anyway. If I defend myself I am attacked. (Lesson 135) You can't know that until you give yourself away. By giving yourself away, you become God's Son, because God only gives. When you give yourself, you create like unto your Creator. Is that nice!

...whether there be tongues, they shall cease... (I Cor 13:8) Finally, proclaiming God is not really true. Come on. Being the savior of the world is not really true. Why would it be? It is only true because you think you need saving. You think it's a big deal to be the savior of the world. It's not a big deal at all.

"How dare you say you are the savior of the world? That you're God Mind? That you are the answer?"

In the movie, "Oh God" the humans do this. They give God all sorts of theological questions to answer, and He answers them perfectly, and they, of course, still deny Him. God works all sorts of miracles, and they still deny Him. It would make absolutely no difference what God would do or say, He would still be denied because the possessions of the human mind are what the denial is. You remember this, guys, I am here representing whole mind, and you are emerging as that. I am telling you that there isn't any such place as this. This is a moment of transition in your own mind from time to eternity. It is a moment that must, and did, occur. Let it happen. I know I am teaching surrender, but doggone it, I don't know what else to do.

Do you think I got this by succeeding? What the hell was I going to succeed in except dying? The only thing I could possibly succeed in would be dying. Isn't that so? I lost!! Thanks be to God! Thank you, Father, for showing me that in my failure was my joy! This is called *A Course In Miracles*. Very early in the *Course*, it says, I know you are not going to like to hear this, but you are in competition with Universal Mind. It says it. You carry a resentment because He won't acknowledge the contest. So you make up other associations in your mind that acknowledge the conflict of your own mind. God doesn't know anything about it. You may still live in this little containment of a battle with yourself if you choose, but the brand new minds that represent the Miracles Healing Center will never acknowledge your ridiculous conflict with, or separation from, God!

Whether there be perceptual knowledge, it will vanish away. (I Cor 13:8) This association is beyond knowing. It does not require any association whatsoever. That's fun, isn't it? Are you happy with that? Are you feeling loving? What are you going to do with it? This is your awakening. It's uncontrollable. But if you let a little reason into your heart along with God's love, that will contain it momentarily to the purpose of spirit, and open to you your entire reason for being here. There is a great deal of real passion in seeing reason. "Where two or more are gathered" is so reasonable to me, I love it! I love the reasonableness that you guys could actually come here and do this. Here you are! Did you just appear here? Did you appear behind closed doors? Do you understand? These doors are closed. There is no one coming in here.

This is the circle of atonement. You are being invited to the totality, you newcomers here, to the experience of the Love of God! That is what the church is, where you come together in that dedication! You come here together as a part of Christ Mind, or Christ's body. But your bodies really aren't separate either. They are just projections of your own mind. As you perfect your body in its Christ association, the body of your affiliates must be enlightened. You can begin to feel how exciting it is for me to be heard at last. This very simple declaration is as old as the mind of man.

For we know in part (because knowledge is a part), *and we prophesy in part…* (I Cor 13:9) because prophecy is the necessity for the idea of a future reference. It is not true, because there is no such thing as a future reference. If the past is gone, there is no future. You cannot prophesy anything except a moment of your return to God. And the Christ did come! Otherwise why are you so excited? Not only that, it is impossible to have an idea of Christ coming, without Him having come anyway! This is the whole *Course In Miracles* and is the entire teaching of singular resurrection. So He came and this world is over? And that's what is freeing you! You are free from a world that is gone. If the world is gone, you would have to be free because you are not here!

But when that which is perfect is come, then that which is in part shall be done away. The whole is not the sum of its parts. *When I was a child, I spake as a child, I understood as a child, I thought as a child: But when I became a man* (grew up into the realization of my mind), *I put away childish things.* (I Cor 13:10-11) This is

59

Chapter 18 of *A Course In Miracles*. I no longer needed to define myself as a man, as a man made by men. I could be whole as a man made by God, or a God-man.

For now we see through a glass, darkly; but then face to face... (I Cor 13:12) Face to face with what? Your own Christhood. What will you look at for a moment? Your own perfection. Why? You were your own particle of darkness. Now you have become your own wave of Love. When you first look at yourself in the mirror of the Light of Life, that is the real world, when you first look at yourself in this mirror, it is very fearful. All these thoughts of fear, which are actually part of your mind, you must and are allowing to reassociate in the new light. For just a moment you will see this beautiful face, then it will dissolve into the ugliness which is in your own mind. This is the practice of *A Course In Miracles*, because you do look through a mirror darkly. It has speckles of form in it; old memories contained within your own mind projected from you. Just as you get the scene of your hologram perfect, an alien will enter in and attack it and destroy it. You have forgotten that he is a part of your own mind. You defended yourself within your own dark mirror. Don't do that.

Let your mirror be a shining reflection of the Son of God which is the Christhood of your body in its re-association of the certainty of your return from time to eternity.

For now we see through a glass, darkly; but then face to face: now I know in part; but then shall I know even as also I am known. (I Cor 13:12) I know even as also I am known, because knowing and being known are the same. I am one Self. This is the entire teaching of enlightenment to reality; from separation to whole singular mind. I am one Self. There is only one Self. I know because God knows. I won't attempt to judge or define. I will accept it as a part of my certainty of my faith in God.

What's being asked of you? That you remember that you are perfect as God created you. What beautiful directions, if you are the cause of the problem! What better direction could I give you than Jesus of Nazareth gives to you when He tells you that you are the cause of the problem?! How simple the solution is if it is true that you are the cause. How impossible the solution is if God is the cause of — or could be aware of — a separation from Himself. It is time to put your toys of death away.

And now abideth faith, hope (expectation), *love/ charity, these three; but the greatest of these is* love/ *charity.* (I Cor 13:13) So you have expectation in Love. You have faith in Love, because God is Love, and the Power of God's Mind is Love. Your faith in the power of God's Mind cannot fail. How simple the solution. Whenever you trust in yourself, you will fail. Trusting in yourself is what failure is. Trusting in yourself is a guarantee of failure, because your reality is based on your necessity to fail.

So this is First Corinthians. Certainly one of the greatest, most lucid, messages of any human mind that ever was. The idea that you come together as a part of the Christ body is perfect. How much it is reduced to some sort of story that we are all separate human beings coming together to share God and His kingdom, I don't know or care. I'm telling you that you are all the same human being coming together. There is only one separation. All of these are but reflections of your own separation. You must accept the atonement for yourself, because the separation is what you are, and the Kingdom of God is what you are. Thank you for coming to the Sunday School class today.

How bright the sanctuary is! There are transformations going on here. Do you want to see how both simple and difficult this is? I have talked about Love. Raise your hand and tell me what I just told you. What have I led you to? An experience of God's Love that is all around you. Without that, without your *Course In Miracles*, it is hopeless. You will just sit there and continue to define and defend yourself.

All this world is, is always only each moment a denial of the Experience of God's Love. All this world is, is always only each moment a denial of the Perfection of you as created by God. Do you understand me? A momentous discovery has occurred. You are determined now — and it is determination, it is an endeavor, and it does give you a real reason for standing here, a real purpose. What reason would you have for standing here if it is not to discover who you are? The admission that you don't know who you are was the fastest way to get there, because you didn't know who you were. You were suffering from the great amnesia of separation. And now, at last, you're awakening!

Your laughing now is the expression of Love. Is Love the freedom from death? Freedom from yourself? Freedom from being a human being? Freedom from suffering the consequences of your meaningless thoughts? Here's some more of First Corinthians: Behold I show you a mystery! In a moment you will be changed. In the twinkling of an eye you will be resurrected. It's all here, isn't it!

What are you seeing here? LOVE. Can you see Love? Can you hear Love? Can you feel Love?

Can you manifest Love in various associations? Yes, but the only thing for sure is that you cannot not be Love! You may manifest it any way that you choose. You can make Love evil as far as I'm concerned. I don't know what good it is going to do you. It only has to do with you in your own mind, anyway. It is only going to be you, no matter what you do. One thing for sure, if you believe you can get sick and die and are a body, you will get sick and die and be a body. You ask me to relieve you from the burden that you have placed on yourself. It is obviously impossible for me to do that. I can offer you the Love of God which we are. If you are determined to hold onto the consequences of your own mind in the historic reference of the separation, there is nothing I can do about it; nor, indeed, can anything in the entire universe. But you cannot make your dream of death a reality.

Perhaps you will believe I am loving you explicitly and that's just fine. But remember, to a whole mind, explicitness is explicitness of the entirety. Obviously all Love here will appear to be a moment of exchange. This is what the miracle is. The miracle is the moment of the exchange with me of your burdensome self for the Love of my mind for you.

But you remember this — our Selves are the same. The Power that we are using is singular; it's the entire Mind of God. When I say myself, I mean my Self. That Self is the same. The manner in which we use that in forgiveness doesn't concern me, because we cannot not be using that power, which is what Love is. Once more: Love is the Power of God Mind. Why are you afraid of Power? Because it is going to attack you and kill you. You are afraid. Power is conflict to you. Power is opposition. Power is defense and attack. But not in reality! Power is Love!

"My body is liable to burn up and disappear." God is a consuming fire of Love! These are the Great Rays. What are you worried about? All you have done is hold yourself in this little place. This is not what you are.

You say, "I'm afraid. I'd better stay in the ultra violet." That's perfectly okay with me. You will have to trust me with this. The universe is nothing but Mind. All I am really offering you is a wide spectrum of energy/Love association. You always narrow your ranges of correspondence in the fear of the passion of you. You are literally afraid of your own creative mind. You feel safe in the security of your definition of your own limitation. That's fine with me. Be secure. But at least stand a moment in this whole new picture of yourself. At least be a whole part of that in your own mind.

No more was ever asked of you than to accept the atonement for yourself, simply because you are the entire conflict. I didn't mean to reduce this, but I want to show you how much more there is to you than you are willing to admit. Your willingness to admit it is what salvation is. There is always more to you than you think there is, even as you discover what everything is. Thinking that you are what everything is, is not what everything is! It is being what everything is!!

The last page of Corinthians says that very unlikely people will come together in the return journey to Heaven. Birds of a feather have a tendency to flock together, and the feathers are the problem.

Human establishment denies eternal life. This is the whole idea that Christ is always with you, and you are always rejecting Him because He doesn't seem to fit into your self-conception. Look at the gathering in this place. These are very unlikely or impossible associations. If you, as a human being, were to look at these apostles with a demand for the recognition of your own credentials, you would say, "What the hell could they possibly find in common?"

What have they found in common? LOVE!!

"How could you possibly claim that?"

It's easy — we Love everything.

Then the world will say, "How dare you love everything unconditionally. I can prove to you that you are dead wrong about this." How can they prove it? They will say, "We will kill you, and then you can't love us. We will prove there is no such thing as total love — we will kill you. Let me see you forgive us when we kill you."

Now, having killed the Christ, they can pretend to acknowledge the saviorship of Jesus who they crucified. They feel very secure because they killed Him when He threatened them with their own perfection through the saving grace of His Love. Suddenly you are appearing with Jesus as a very major threat to them, so this world must crucify you to keep itself from Love.

Be of good cheer. The whole place and everything in it is only an old disappearing nightmare of yours anyway. What a wonderful assignment you've accepted and become — Mission Impossible!!

Welcome to the end of this world in the exact place and moment of its misconceived beginning.

Welcome Home.

And though I bestow all my goods to feed the poor,
and though I give my body to be burned,
and have not charity, it profiteth me nothing.
Charity suffereth long, and is kind, charity envieth not,
charity vaunteth not itself, is not puffed up,
Doth not behave itself unseemly, seeketh not her own,
is not easily provoked, thinketh no evil,
Rejoiceth not in iniquity, but rejoiceth in the truth,
Beareth all things, believeth all things,
hopeth all things, and endureth all things.
Charity never faileth,
but whether there be prophecies, they shall fail,
whether there be tongues, they shall cease,
whether there be knowledge, it shall vanish away.
For we know in part, and we prophesy in part.
But when that which is perfect is come,
then that which is in part shall be done away.
When I was a child, I spake as a child,
I understood as a child, I thought as a child,
but when I became a man, I put away childish things
For now we see through a glass, darkly,
but then face to face, now I know in part,
but then shall I know even as also I am known.
And now abideth faith, hope, charity, these three,
but the greatest of these is charity.

- I Corinthians 13

The Healing Power of Love

And the greatest of them all is charity. Welcome. We are coming together here, under the auspices of the message of my savior Jesus Christ, to attempt in a particular way, to convey to each other an idea of Love. We began this episode with some lovely messages from Corinthians 13, with the idea that it would be possible for us, at this time, to give total value to the idea of Love.

In our *Course In Miracles*, at the very onset, we began to look together at the idea that I can't teach you the meaning of Love because that is beyond what can be taught. And the reason that it is beyond what can be taught is that we are Love. If I appear here in a garb of human conception, based on an idea of an illusion of correspondence in separation, I cannot *not* be offering you Love, because God is Love.

Practice: "God is Love." The lessons that come after 170 in the workbook of *A Course In Miracles* are going to instruct you to say: "God is but Love, and therefore so am I." And when you catch the Old Man...They call me the Old Man, because having undergone the devastating experience of my own annihilation in correspondence with my body, I discovered to my incredible amazement that I was surrounded by the light of Love. And, for many other teachers of God, through the resurrection of themselves in recognition of the transfiguration of the energy of the body, beginning to teach Love, within fleshy tones of vibrations of light, is a manner in which we convey to each other in instantaneous communication in the idea that we are wholly contained within aspects of what the Universe is, and can share within the entirety of that relationship any one single moment of communication, which is God's Love.

"And I give to you, as you give to me, true Love." Is Love what Truth is? In the translations from the Aramaic, the performance of the act of Love is termed, as we read you in Corinthians, "charity." The highest act that can be performed by the human condition in a re-association with itself, is the *act* of giving. Listen carefully: It is not in the observation of what has been given, so that you can obtain an idea of exchange contained within the possession of Love. Practice: "Love does not possess." What would it possess? Itself? So, contained in the idea of the act of the giving, or the sharing of Love, is the certainty that we are that. Not more than that, not in the idea of being puffed up with definitions of yourself. Not less than that, in the false humility that identifies your determination not to see the wholeness of you in the relationship with the universe, but rather the simple admission that you are whole and perfect as you were created, and, in a particular sense, can only love. We do have the dilemma of your need to define yourself as other than Love. Since you are the totality of God creating, your definition of yourself is a retention, momentarily, within space/time, of the conflict you feel in the need to define yourself as other than that. Protect everything that you value by that simple act.

Here I come; I am going to begin to convey a little Love to you. Along with this conveyance of Love will go my certainty of a healing process, wherein I can take the fleshiness of you, the natural man of you, the you that maintains it is yourself in its suffering of maintenance, and show you that in a moment of conveyance of recognition of each other we see our own wholeness and are healed and whole.

Many of the earlier videos that I have done convey to you the essence of the Truth — that if Love is the power of Mind, the power that I offer you concerning my own self-realization is the power of Love. Now, the simplicity of the application of Love often escapes the human condition, very simply because of the need of the application. Objectively you formulate in your own minds an idea about objective Love, and you place it outside yourself and utilize it together as a definition of the correspondence you have found in the retention of your separation. And while you may do that, what's going to occur? If you have ideas about yourself being in Love, and share the isolation of objective reality within the matrix of light, you will use up the causation of you, based on the effects that you value within your own relationship with yourself. Since the cause of the Universe is the Mind of God and since God is Love, you obviously can't use up your Love, even including your human Love — even including the idea that you could communicate together with each other.

I Love you. Now does that mean that I have rejected this other association within my mind? Do I Love you then to the exclusion of someone who appears to be in the propinquity of association of objective reality (we call that neighbor)? Is a neighbor other than the one that I Love? Yet I have learned, through the mind training of this *Course* of the power of extension of my mind, simply to give away my objective associations, since the meaning of myself lies only in the extension thereof.

Yes. Here... May I share that with you? I am going to read you just a little bit, with your permission, from one of the books (called *Jesus is Speaking)* of the certainty that the miracle is being performed in our hearts and minds

Why is it important that you hear it? Say to me: "Jesus *is* Speaking!"

Say it again. Yes. The Christ in you, the idea of your perfection, the determination on your part to express yourself as whole and perfect, is the basis of the New Testament of Jesus. OK?

Thou shalt Love thy neighbor as thyself. Shall we look once more at why the necessity for that is so pertinent in our ideas of our association? Our neighbor is an idea about our self. If I have an idea about myself in a constant reminder of my capacity to remain within a frame of space/time that will continually be altered by the Light and Love of God, I can remain in a constancy of presenting to you a healed body.

The miracle healers, the Christian healers that are utilizing the mind of Jesus — which is nothing but the Christ Mind, which becomes their own mind as they take on the burden of the extension of their Christianity (of their own saviorship) — discovered to their amazement that greater things will they do than were performed by Jesus, because he has ascended and now is offering the entirety of the solution, outside of the frame of the memory patterns of containment that previously represented your body form.

As we appear now in this idea of the conversion of our minds, we are communicating instantly in recognition that any distance between us, using the speed of light, will deny us access to the entirety of communication.

Look with me. If I intend to love you out of here — and many of you are sharing this, and you are sharing it with me now — I could not make distinctions between what appears to be one body and what appears to be the other body. Now the grievance you might feel in your separate associations with each other, is that I have confessed my Love for this association. You now have a grievance of jealousy in the possibility of your loss of the possessions that we share within the limitations we impose on ourselves in order to justify our own death, or our own annihilation. Love can only be freedom of our self - recognition, because Love is what freedom from the bondage of pain and death is.

I am going to read you just one little passage from the New Testament of Jesus that pertains directly to the offering that we are sharing. Listen:

What you fear is nothing. There is nothing to fear. There is nothing covered that shall not be revealed and hid that shall not be known.

Look: *What I tell you in darkness that speak you in light, and what you hear in the ear, that preach you upon the housetops.*

Yet a little while and the world will see you no more but I will see you, and because I live you shall live also! Now you will know that I am in my Father, and you are in me and I in you.

Since you have loved me and kept my words, my Father will love you. And we will come unto you and make our abode with you.

And now that you abide in me, my words abide in you. Ask what you will and it shall be given unto you.

As the Father has loved me, so have I loved you. Continue you in my love.

You have kept my commandments, and you shall abide in my love. Even as I have kept my Father's commandments and abide in his love.

These things have I spoken unto you, that my joy might remain in you that your joy might be full.

Remember from Jesus: *You have not chosen me but I have chosen you, and I have ordained you. And This is my commandment...* Are you listening? *That you love one another, as I have loved you.*

Love me as I have loved you. Let's look at some of the difficulties that we may encounter in attempting to love each other in our body association. If I appear before you as a body identity, it's impossible you will not see me within the projection of your own idea of body form and hold me in the bondage of what we would term a unique attempt to correspond not utilizing the power of Love. Yet all power is given unto you in heaven and in earth, so that we may share together the power that is God's gift to us, in the certainty that an idea of the totality of yourself, in relationship both with God and with the conceptual idea of the formulation of space/time, is actually, in a single moment of entirety, all that there really is.

So much of the joy that you are feeling with me, as what you term a "Master Teacher", who appears before you in an association of the correspondence of time, offers you evidence of the power of a moment of exchange, where you allow a penetration into your determination to defend yourself within the matrix of non-communicative ideas held in the retention of location. You experience an expansion and feel the joy of the light of you that came with you into the idea of separation, so that the performance of the act of Love would heal our sick relationships with each other that previously defined our need to be separate bodies and suffer the consequences within a time frame that doesn't allow us to see that surrounding us is the whole Kingdom and Love of God.

And what I am trying to show you, by a reasoning process in my mind is that as available to you as is available to me is, let's call it "the Christ Mind" — the Whole Mind, the Self-realization of the Singular Reality that expresses a moment of communication with each other.

Communication,— direct communication— will always be a threat to your body constitution, because it will be a momentary loss of the retention of a matrix of energy-form that in the highest truth can be expressed as non-communicative. That is, there is absolutely no reason for this world at all, including the necessity for the illusion thereof. So that when I offer you the power of mind to undergo the entirety of an experience, it will be a re-cellularization of the formulation of the molecular association of your body.

I have a promise here. There was a call, from one of my very dear loved ones who is suffering from — what do you call that, arthritis? The idea that you are a body and undergoing an aging process... Let's use me as a good example of a seventy-seven year-old body, who obviously isn't seventy-seven. Shall I tell you why? There is no such thing as a body. Within the matrix of light energy, you actually believe that we have separate bodies in our association.

Listen with me, Martha: The healing that I am about to perform in regard to your arthritis will simply be my recognition of you as whole and perfect. How can I recognize you as whole and perfect? You *are* whole and perfect! Need I tell you that all power is given unto you in heaven and earth for you to have an experience of the healing of that arthritis? I will if you want me to. There is no need for you to suffer that association of the pain that you are feeling in regard to that idea that these limbs will become withered and that that body is going to be contained, as you undergo the loss of a frequency of the determination to stay specialized within your own body relationship.

You want to use me? These are the Christian healers that are going out into the world, using the power of the Mind of Jesus to heal, and the Spirit of the energy of the association of a new correspondence of body identity — not concerned about their concepts at all. Look with me. This *Course* teaches us that if we will momentarily release the identity of separate body associations, we will have an experience of direct communication. There it was! Here, look. Ha…hoo! Now, do these hands appear to be those of a seventy-six year old man? Say to me: "You are just an illusion." So, I am just an illusion. You look with me at this. If you want to believe you're a…I think on the last video I told you I fell in love with you because you were a sixty year old or sixty-eight or fifty or forty year old body identity, that I recognized with our minds.

Love communicates, and nothing else communicates. What I am offering you is your capacity… Shall I tell you where you fear this? You have an inborn capacity, or ability — say to me: — "to fall in Love." Fall in Love. How fearful you are of the idea of a complete falling in Love! It will be a momentary loss of the definition of yourself in retention of the idea that you can love separate from the power of the Universe.

Everyone watching this video, I hope, is about to have an experience of falling in Love. Shall I tell you why? Falling in Love is what healing is. Since God only loves, I protect all of my need for disease and arthritis simply by giving it away. As I give it, in the thoughts of my own mind, it is converted to an agency of instant light communication within the power of the Universe.

Is that too simplistic for you? That's too bad! The mind that I am offering you is, are you ready? —Ageless. Because Universal Love knows not of age. Love knows not of death. Love knows not of the associations of the fleshiness of your body, but rather sees us together in this moment of communication.

So Love goes with us wherever we go, because Love is the Mind of God with which we think. I'll be right back. A reminder that… I think I am falling in Love. And the healing that occurred, that I had promised to that association, is joyfully being experienced as a wholeness in relationship with the correspondence both of time and space.

God bless us, each and everyone. I'll see you in a minute.

* * * * * * *

So we are encountering each other in a moment of Love. And since this is the only real moment that we have, we have a choice either to love each other, which would be a major confession of our inability to deal with the chaos of this world or… And the moment that we didn't attempt to find correspondence in our objective association with each other, our body is healed. Can you see this with me? The reason our body is healed is our body is an illusion of a correspondence of a light factor that at no single moment actually exists. It is a matrix of light energy that I can give a moment of constancy if you

75

won't protect yourself from the fear that you have of the entirety of the encounter.

Let's practice, just for a moment, the idea of power of mind. There… there it was. The experience that we just shared was a moment of recognition of the power of the Universal Mind of God, based on a process of giving. Remember at the beginning of the video where we stressed, through Paul, how important the idea of charity is? The associations with Love, in the action of self-recognition, is the entirety of a moment of giving. Shall we practice together some giving? *I'll give to you, as you give to me, true Love.* Look. I use the power of the Love of God to define our re-association together, without the need to remain in the constriction of the matrix of light energy that appears to be your location in time.

Look with me. God only gives. There. Now, you begin to relax your defenses of self-identity, because it was your need to hold yourself in self-identity that prevented you from loving. Because, by possessing ideas about yourself, within your own mind, you restricted the eternal process of the power of a single mind to find the totality of itself in its own effects. So that any idea of containment denies access to creative reality.

Will you listen with me just a little bit about the power of our individual encounters with each other, and how fearful you are of a direct encounter with me? I am looking at you conceptually. I am very certain that you intend to protect yourself within that body form. And I am just as certain, if you utilize the concepts of your mind to remain in definition of yourself, you will be a correspondence of our bodies. You will then find me in a formulation within the matrix that justifies our separate body associations.

I am going to remind you of something very important. You can hear this: The continuity of the correspondences of our minds and our ideas about ourselves are not sequential. Remember the practice that we did on this last video from chapter 28 of the *Text*? Let's practice it together — because I can see that you are about to have that experience. There is no link of our memory in association with each other, at this moment, to our old association. So that if I come here... Come on... I am going to be a seventy-seven year old body... Shall I try it with you? I think I'll try it with you. I am going to be a seventy-seven year old man...I don't know how to do that! You will have to help me with that. Look at me there, you! I am going to give you all my Love and demand to know why you want to stay that body. I am very much aware that you are going to utilize that arthritis that you previously had, in order to associate yourself with a body. You will then find the necessity to overcome the pain of arthritis, rather than simply admitting that all of the pain being manifest in this world is being caused within your own mind, and that as you change your mind this world will change.

Look with me: I am going, and intend, to see you whole and perfect within the mind that we share with God — whether you like it or not. And while you are hell-bent on retaining your experience of your determination to justify your own location and, hence, your necessity of non-communicative effects of what was previous in your past association that disallow you to see the present condition that I am offering you, so will it be with you.

If all power is given unto you in heaven and earth — you right there — nothing in the Universe can prevent you from organizing your conceptual associations in your determination to remain within this little (how does our savior term it?) "infinite maze of nothingness of dark energy", that you will not allow me to penetrate with my

Love. Because if you begin to fall in Love, you will lose your necessity to defend yourself from the eternal Love of God, and collapse completely into Love.

Practice: "Let's collapse into Love together." I saw your fear come in. "Yes, but what am I going to do?" Do you see what you are afraid of? Let's share together a real fundamental thing: Say to me, "I am afraid of the Love of God." Of course! How would you not be? Jesus says, "There is nothing to be afraid of, and when you are fearful, you are nothing." Now, what occurs in the association with nothing and nothing, within the matrix, obviously, could not concern my mind, because I am the light of the world. Who is the light of the world? You are!

Would you want to practice with me a minute? Say to me: "I am the light of the world." You won't even say it? [laughs] You're really going to protect yourself, aren't you? There is no requirement that you believe it, because your beliefs are what you use as standards of denial. But the admission of the light of the world can come to you in self-recognition. Shall I tell you why? You are the light of the world! But belief is strong indeed, so the practice of our minds is to make the declaration, because the energy of the Universe can enter in to a moment of shared Love.

I am going to read you just a little bit from our book called: *Jesus is Speaking*. And it is from our *Course in Miracles*, but it's an activation of the idea of the experience we are having together, and that we just had right there. My goodness sake! Listen to me: The healing that occurred in regard to that arthritis... Come on, don't you tell me that hand is seventy-seven years old — come on! "Well it is all wrinkled" So what does that mean? You have given your hand an idea about what you are within your own mind. Ahhhh...

Say to me: "I wish what you were teaching me were true." Good. Good. Because in your expression of desire was your need for another solution. Because sure as hell —and you are in hell— the idea that you're that body can not *not* give you the result of being a body. And that will mean that you are going to have to occupy that little place in space/time until you degenerate and turn to dust, into the nothing of momentary correspondence of the idea of your separation, which I am denying you at this moment.

You made a bargain to die. You want to trust me with this? All of the bargaining that goes on in this world is based on your determination to suffer the consequences of our conflict in correspondence with each other.

Listen: Defend everything you value by the act of giving it away. The Love that I am feeling for you is nothing but the freedom of my mind to utilize the power of light that surrounds me and that I was previously fearful of. And in the devastating idea of the conversion of my mind, in the ordeal of being reborn, we will recognize each other in a new matrix of light energy in which our communication becomes instantaneous. Ok? To give and receive are one in truth, because *I am the light of the world.* Say it. There it was. When you gave, you recognized immediately in the act of giving, the entirety of the association. Because in the lesson, what did we learn? You can only give to yourself. Say that to me. Yes. All of the images that represent your objective association, that appear to surround you, define your poverty of self-containment in which you attempt to possess the idea of limitation, in order to gain in the abundance of the limitation you impose on yourself in order to define yourself in that location.

How impoverished you are in the idea of Love through protection! How much the idea of a moment of Love is lost in your determination to contain it in an idea of the necessity for self-termination! Indeed, Love is letting go of fear. Look. The only thing that could possibly be retained by you, within your own concept, is an idea of fear. Can you see it with me?

Let's look real quickly together about the offering within the containment of your own self-identity that is now penetrated into the illusion of location, so that we can see together that I will represent to you a character within your own dream of separation, who heretofore you were fearful of letting come into an arrangement of correspondence in space/time, even though you expressed a need for the idea of Jesus. The idea that the Christ is standing next to you in your own mind, caused you to withdraw deeper into the idea of fear to the point where you finally asked for the help that I am intending to offer you.

So much of our attention has been given... As I looked at your world today... I came back into this association yesterday; I am going to be here today and I will be leaving tomorrow. So much of what is going on within your matrix is expressing your necessity to protect yourself, that for many of you it's become ludicrous. Everything that represents you appears to be a need to protect yourself — to the point where you say, "I've had enough of this." You ask for the power of the Universe that is inherent in you, and you receive it in the correspondence of your need for it. Knock, and it will be opened. But you are afraid it is going to be opened, because you are not certain what is behind the door. I can assure you that if you know what is behind the door, you will retain it in the idea of correspondence with yourself and deny yourself access to a portal that, while it appears to you to be dark, is actually shining in readiness for you just beyond your own event horizon of containment.

So the moment of falling in Love is a collapse of your body form, from which will emerge "the ashes of the Phoenix", we used to call it. You'll take on new aspects of degrees and intervals found within the matrix of light energy that previously separated you. We just fell together. Yes I will read a little bit.

Listen: *The light has come.* Lesson 75 — Seventy-five days into the idea of this mind training and suddenly we are penetrating the darkness of your human correspondence. There is a lot of excitement going on about our *Course In Miracles.* What happens is, in the repetition of the idea of your perfection, even though you have no idea of even really entertaining the idea that all power is given to you in heaven and earth, the expression of it increases the faith in the idea of a single Source of Reality, which is really what you are.

The emphasis on this *Course In Miracles* for your conceptual self-identities is very simply that you need do nothing. You don't have to do anything in order to identify yourself as perfect. But in the loss of your need to find correspondence in exchange, you'll fall in Love entirely. And everyone in this world will look at you and the foolishness of your dedication to establish a new innocence about yourself in your relationship with the Universe.

I am whole and perfect as I was created. I cannot suffer loss; there is nothing that can happen to me that can cause me a confusion of identity, unless I am determined that it occur.

Suddenly Love is surrounding us, isn't it, and Love is becoming the mind with which we think, the manner in which we communicate with each other. Why? The light has come. The power of the Love of God is expressed in a moment of light. Are you listening to me there, human condition? I am teaching you that Love is the enlightenment of your mind; without regard to who you thought you were in the definition of yourself.

To you, the idea that you're whole and perfect is the epitome of the ego's determination not to recognize your perfection, for fear of your necessity to perform acts of healing, utilizing the power of the Love of God rather than your own containment, in which case this world is going to deny you and attack you very simply because you are declaring the totality of Love in a new-found association we have with each other.

The light has come, you are whole and you can heal. Listen: *The light has come, You are healed and you can heal. The light has come, You are saved and you can save. You are at peace, and you bring peace with you wherever you go. Darkness and turmoil and death have disappeared.* Why? *The light has come. Today we celebrate the happy ending to your long dream of disaster. There are no dark dreams now.*

Why? Say to me: "The light has come." Good. *Today the time of light begins for you and for everyone. It is a new era, in which a new world is born. The old one has left no trace upon it in its passing. Today we will see a different world, because the light has come.*

The light has come. You are healed and you are whole. And I saw you begin to express it in this exchange.

Look with me: The practice of the idea of an alternative within the matrix of death has gained momentum in your mind, very simply because the Love of God surrounds you, and it's what you are. No, not some other body. You.

Say to me, "The salvation of the world depends on me." I'll help you. You don't want to say it? You have to say it. At least give me a conceptual advantage in the idea you might begin to practice the mind training that will allow you to see the power that is actually yours in this little idea of being endowed inherently with your escape from the prison of the correspondence of light that has held you in the idea of potential, or containment within the dark idea of the non-utilization of the Source of Reality. A moment of disaster that I have led you directly to — and you are beginning to enjoy the conversion of disaster without your need to retain it within the idea of correspondences of sequential time.

Listen to one more sentence: *The light has come. I have forgiven the world.*

Dwell not upon the past today. Look. *Keep a completely open mind, washed of all past ideas and clean of every concept that you have made. You have forgiven the world today and You can look upon it now as if you never saw it before.* Because you never did see it before. *You do not know yet what it looks like. You merely wait to have it shown to you. And while you wait, repeat several times, slowly and in complete patience, The light has come. I have forgiven the world.*

Realize that your forgiveness entitles you to vision. Understand that the Holy Spirit never fails to give the gift of sight to the forgiving. Believe He will not fail you now. You have forgiven the world. He will be with you as you watch and wait. He will show you what true vision sees. It is His Will, You have joined with Him. So, *wait patiently for Him. He will be there. Because The light has come. And You have forgiven the world.*

That was one of the fastest fifty-seven minutes that I have ever experienced within the idea that you'd let me come into your correspondence. Will you share something with me? The idea that the light has penetrated in your defenses is nothing but the admission of the totality of the requirement for the metamorphosis of your mind in association with correspondences of time. You will perform the act of rebirth, very simply because you are the act of rebirth.

So what did we learn in this first fifty-seven minutes? (It was actually a period of almost three hundred years.) We learned that each time we found a correspondence outside of our self that justified the longevity of our body form, we could live out, over a period of twenty years or fifty or a hundred or a thousand or seventy-seven years, the idea that we were separate from reality. But each time we allowed the penetration of the light to enter in, we shortened our necessity to defend ourselves within the idea of the objective separation that justified our need to terminate our self.

We leave you with this. The light has come into your mind sufficiently so you no longer are attracted to the idea of self-termination in location.

One more look at the conflict of this world and you'll decide. Though you are not certain what the alternative is, you'll wait patiently, just for a moment, for it to occur.

Because we are very certain that God goes with us wherever we go, being the Mind with which we are thinking, in which we found this correspondence of healing that represents our Love for each other.

I'll come back and do one more hour all about this new experience of Love that we're sharing together. And as we say together, "God bless us, each and everyone," we recognize that in that moment of blessing, we are whole and perfect, and Love takes over as a manifestation of what we really are, in awakening from this dream. I'll see you in a minute.

[End of First Hour]

* * * * * * *

This is an invitation to a great experiment. Just for a moment, lay aside the prejudices of your human establishment and listen to these words with your heart. Listen with your heart. Listen again, and still again. Just for a moment, let this simple message of truth and love be beyond all reason and see how quickly reason will follow as your mind opens to the joyful light of your reunion with the eternally creating mind of God.

Whoever you think you are, wherever you appear to be in the desperate sea of chaos that is this world, let the breath of this timeless voice of resurrected mind rekindle in you the ancient memory of your own perfect reality. Now are you being called to fulfill the only purpose that ever could have been given for your sojourn into this meaningless world of loneliness and death. That purpose is your escape from it through the message of salvation that is now in your hands.

The message of salvation is now in your hands. And the certainty that I am offering you, based on my own illumination of mind through my heartfelt need for a solution, will allow you to find correspondences within our minds because any single whole mind that hears this will represent, within the entirety of the matrix of separation, a moment of self-realization. That's why the salvation of the world depends on you. Will you say that to me? Yes. Not to the world.

In this message from my savior Jesus, he didn't come to save the world, he didn't come to have anything to do with the world, he didn't come to judge the world, he didn't come to condemn it, he certainly didn't come to condemn you because of the isolation of the guilt you feel in regard to yourself. He came to tell you that you have been chosen by him to represent the entirety of the conversion of light form. You are the light bearer, and you brought this light with you. In that other hour we said that light is now in you and we expect you to use it. And we expect you to carry it back to where it was given to you in the certainty, as we just read you, that you rekindle the idea of the entirety of the solution to your problem that was momentarily lost in the displacement of your mind.

So much of our *Course* is based on the realignment that just occurred there. I am coming in here as what you call the Master Teacher; I am in a process of realigning this world. The idea that I would be concerned about the concepts of the limitation of your body form are beyond ridiculous. They have no meaning. The whole basis of our *Course* is to teach you the relinquishment of the concept of your self-identity. Your self-identity, within the idea of dark form, within the dream of death, is what's holding you in the bondage of your body form.

The real problem you have is, if you don't reject me right about now, you're actually going to have to entertain within your own idea of sequential time what I am offering you in your own salvation, or the certainty that the problem of this world is contained only within your own identity of yourself. And that the solution is nothing but the release of your defenses of your idea of who you're not.

Human, in your own dream, you will not be successful at the retention of self-will, because it is not the Will of God that you suffer from pain and death. The will of this world is the denial of your perfection. Remember about Love? Some of us have attempted... I saw you...We have a class that wrote me a beautiful letter about coming together to practice unconditional Love. The reason that unconditional Love is difficult to practice is because you will have a notion in your concepts that there are some conditions out there that you have to practice forgiving. Do you see how difficult that becomes for you? You will then believe — this is a message directly from Jesus — that it is actually necessary for you to forgive the objective associations of pain and fear that you are hell-bent on holding on to, in order to justify yourself.

The offering that I am giving you, concerning Love, is not unconditional in the sense that you must give up the condition that caused the fear, but rather that you turn and, through a moment of forgiveness, represent to yourself the entirety of your determination of self-identity that has denied you access to the Creative Source. Yes, of course, this is Sermon on the Mount.

The whole nature of my teaching to you is that the Universe is thought, and that any single thought of Love, if we won't interfere with it conceptually, will express our Love for each other. I am appearing in the illusion of a seventy-seven year old body, and if you are looking at me from your age perspective and can't see that I am not contained in the body, you will not be able to see the immediacy of a correspondence in another matrix of energy that's going on beside us.

Ask not the sparrow how the eagle soars. Those who are determined to reflect back to themselves correspondences of body association, in a literal sense, will not be able to share in the power of our individual minds to heal the sick and raise the dead, as we have been instructed to do by the savior of this world, who represents himself as Jesus of Nazareth and now requires that through the light and Love you feel for each other, you express your certainty of the only possible reason that you could be here — and that's to escape from this matrix of death.

Let's look together, just for a moment, at the idea of the immediacy of the possibility of correspondence within this containment. We have forty-two minutes to go, in the entirety of your identity of coming in to the idea of death and leaving. If you will accept from me the certainty that the time is not actually passing, all of the memories that come into your mind of fear can be converted to Love, very simply because you have been depending on the passion of fear to retain Love. And the idea of a fearful Love really doesn't make any sense. But the encounter you are having with me — this from the beautiful text of Jesus — can show you that our encounter, while it contains all of the conflict of our separation, can be converted instantly.

Listen: *Glory to God in the highest, and to you because He has so willed it. Ask and it shall be given you, because it has already been given. Ask for light and learn that you are light. If you want understanding and enlightenment you will learn it, because your decision to learn it is the decision to listen to the Teacher Who knows of light, and can therefore teach it to you.* Listen: *There is no limit on your learning because there is no limit on your mind. There is no limit on His teaching because He was created to teach. Understanding His function perfectly He fulfills it perfectly, because that is His joy and yours.*

And my function is — if you are going to allow me to teach you — is only to show you the enjoyment we can share in our escape. Say to me "Hell." Yes, you are in hell. What else would a matrix of dark form of your containment be, if it is not hell?

We are reading from Chapter 8 of the text of *A Course In Miracles* about an instant of a holy encounter that will allow you to change your mind about what you want to be your direction. If you are determined that your direction be to retain the idea of separation within the conflict of the power of your own mind, so will it be. The moment that you would ask for the entirety of the solution, time will collapse in on you in an idea of a miracle, which shortens your necessity to participate in the illusion of separation. It acts as a catalyst, breaking up erroneous ideas that you have about yourself. Do you see that? Now, those of you who just had that experience of joy: All you did was look back into yourself and say to yourself, "Wait a minute, there's got to be another way. The world I see holds nothing that I want. My meaningless thoughts are showing me a meaningless world. I am holding a grievance about myself because what I see out there is totally meaningless, yet I am determined to give it meaning."

And the practice of this *Course* has begun to come to fruition in the idea that indeed we can escape, the idea that I am not going to hold that grievance any longer.

I looked at your world this morning. You want to share something with me? I am in your mind now, in your heart and hopefully we have a body association — I don't know how you can stand it! I looked into your nightmare. I see how determined you are to represent yourself as that body, as though somehow, something outside of yourself, over which you had no control, was going to continue to perpetrate the idea of the sinfulness of your separation. It is not true. It is not true. Sleeping one: This is an Advent of a Great Awakening. It's the idea that we can share moments of revelation, based on a single revelation that brought about a resurrection of our body form. This, our message from Jesus.

It is a *holy* encounter because it's a *whole* encounter. Look: You can't encounter yourself partially. If you do, you will share the conflict of your partiality for the retention of your separation and condemn your brother to the same mis-identity that justifies your idea about yourself.

This is a holy encounter. Somewhere in your sojourn in time you have encountered me. And though it may not have been your particular decision at that time to do it, it's impossible that somewhere in time you're not going to meet the entirety of your own solution, because the entirety of your own solution is who you are — if it is true that you are only meeting yourself, not a "partialization" of yourself that condemns your brother to the mis-representation that fosters your need to be that body.

Practice: "I am not a body." You're encountering a light factor of illusion that appears to be an old guy, within your matrix of identity of memory. And you are in a repetition of conflict. I looked at your war — what's going on as you prepare to retain the conflict and pretend that it is Love. I watch you establish ideas of conflict to which you enclose yourself in the idea of possession and call it Love. You then suffer the idea of the passion of conflict that justifies your idea of Love.

Enough of that foolishness! I have had plenty of experiences in regard to the necessity for utilizing the idea of revenge as a solution to my problem, only to discover that no matter how much revenge I sought and obtained, I could not be happy. It occurred to me suddenly within the entirety of the idea of myself the necessity for forgiveness, even though I had no intention of forgiving. I didn't need an intention of forgiving for it to be applicable. Because in truth — are you going to listen to me for a moment then I'll read this — there isn't anything to forgive. There isn't anything out there that is going to require your forgiveness within the conflict of your own mind. The encounter that I am offering you, if you'll allow it to occur, will simply spread the light that you brought with you when you came, so that you can fulfill the function you were designed to do, having been chosen to enter into the mission of salvation with the dedication to perform the act that you momentarily have forgotten.

The great amnesia of this world — not knowing who you are, or why you are here, or what you are doing — is about to disappear now as the light and Love that we share together finds a new correspondence in a new continuity of time where we begin to laugh at the idea that this world is what life is.

Look: You came here to die. And you will die until you change your mind. All I can do in this mind training is offer you the certainty of my Love for you, not in death, but in the recognition of life. *There is no death.* Say it. *The Son of God is free. Swear not to die you holy Son of God. You made a bargain* — with the idea of this body form — *you can't keep.* I am threatening you with an encounter, a devastating act of the admission of your own falsity. Good for you!

Listen: *To fulfill the Will of God perfectly is the only joy and peace that can be fully known, because it is the only function that can be fully experienced. When this is accomplished, then, there is no other experience. Yet the wish for other experience will block its accomplishment, because God's Will cannot be forced upon you, being an experience of total willingness.* Say it again: "God's Will is an experience of total willingness." Now, *The Holy Spirit understands how to teach this, but you do not. That is why you need Him, and why God gave Him to you. Only His teaching will release your will to God's, uniting it with His power and glory and establishing them as yours. You share them as God shares them, because this is the natural outcome of their being.*

The Will of the Father and the Son are One, by Their extension. Their extension is the result of Their Oneness, holding Their unity together by extending Their joint Will. Look: *This is perfect creation by the perfectly Created, in union with the perfect Creator. The*

Father must give Fatherhood to His Son, because His own Fatherhood must be extended outward. Look: *You who belong in God, have the holy function of extending His Fatherhood by placing no limits upon it. Let the Holy Spirit teach you how to do this, for you can know what it means only of God Himself.*

One more paragraph: *When you meet anyone remember it is a holy encounter. And as you see him, you will see yourself. As you treat him, you will treat yourself. As you think of him, you will think of yourself. Never forget this, for in him you will find yourself or lose yourself. Whenever two Sons of God meet, they are given another chance at salvation. Do not leave anyone without giving salvation to him and receiving it yourself.* This is from Jesus: *For I am always there with you in remembrance of you.*

We are in an encounter. Aren't we? I am encountering you somewhere in time. And you are encountering me. Will you share this with me? We have met before. The problem we have with meeting before is, in the simple truth of the matter, we can only meet here and now. Yet we can hold memories of having met before in the conflict of the retention of the hatred that we feel in the grievance that we have against God and, in fact, the whole world.

Are you still holding a grievance against me? Of course. The condition of a human being is a grievance against everything. The idea that you would hold a grievance, in the loss of your need to justify yourself, can only give you a particular, in which you will believe that the power of the Universe is in conflict. And since the conflict is in your own mind, you cannot *not* believe that you are somewhere within an idea of pain and loneliness and death that constitutes your apparent reality. And it is not true.

I have come into a world that does deny itself everything. This is directly from the scripture of Jesus. Yet I can only offer that certainty to you individually, because the world is a product of the grievance that you hold in your inability to locate yourself.

The idea of grievance is paramount in the idea of forgiveness because without the idea of forgiveness you cannot know that the entirety of the grievance lies within your own mind. So that the lesson that we did, pertaining to the light has come and you are healed and can heal, will attempt to show you in a subsequent lesson that it's the grievance within your own conceptual mind that denies you access to the light. Two minutes about it:

Love Holds No Grievances. You who were created by love like itself can hold no grievance and know your Self. To hold a grievance is to forget who you are. To hold a grievance is to see yourself as a body. To hold a grievance is to let the ego rule your mind and to condemn the body to death.

Perhaps you do not yet fully realize just what holding grievances does to your mind. It seems to split you off from your Source and make you unlike Him. It makes you believe that He is like what you think you have become, for no one can conceive of His Creator as unlike himself. And that's the whole problem you have with the grievance you are holding against me.

Our first half hour in this second hour is going to be up in approximately two minutes. I expect you, in that two minutes, to forgive the reflections of your own mind by offering you the certainty of my Love. Shall we practice that I am falling in Love with you? And that may make you grieve. But the only reason that you could grieve about the power of us to share our Love together is because of your fear that that's true. Every time we say "I Love you" to each other we have a tendency to examine, within our own grievances, how that could possibly be true. Are you listening with me? Within our own grievances it's not true. All this lesson really shows you is that the condemnation is not out there but within our own minds. I have no concern about your body function. I could care less about how your conceptual formulation has caused you to think that you're that rotting carcass of nothingness, contained within a matrix of light form that denies you the entirety of the reality — which you are about to experience through our Love for each other.

Now, the action of that moment of encounter is what the Love of God is. The healing that just occurred there I am delighted to see because it's a healing that came about from our minds and had nothing to do with our bodies.

I'll be back in just a minute. We've got twenty-seven minutes to go.

Remember that God goes with us wherever we go and all of that power of light that surrounds us has shortened the entirety of your sojourn to the next twenty-seven minutes. Let's say it together, "God bless us, each and everyone" and stand by for a holy encounter.

* * * * * * *

God, thank you for showing me that I am whole and perfect as You created me.

The bright power of these words of prayer spoken for you and by you, in the name of Jesus Christ is far beyond any dim idea within the darkness of your human identity. Look: *Nothing in this world can even remotely compare to the joyous healing experience possible through the application of God's Love they will provide as you speak them.* We want you to use these words now and depend on them. *These prayers are an immediate direct communicating link between this isolated place of pain, and loss and death and the certain freedom of eternal life that is the Universal Love of God.* [Introduction to *Jesus Is Praying*]

So I am back with you and you caught me reading from the "Jesus is Praying book." What is going to astound you in this re-communication that we have established is the nature of what prayer actually is. You suffer from a dilemma of getting the result of your own mind. The problem is not that. The problem is, since you have no idea who you are, or what you are doing, the moment you get the result within the reflection of yourself, you don't want it. And the reason you don't want it is because the results you're getting are actually rejections of your own mind that you put outside of yourself and retain in a grievance for gratification of your inability to solve the problem. Shall I tell you why, conceptual mind, human being? You don't want the problem solved because the conflict of your own mind, in your self-identity, is what you are. And if I come to fulfill the prophecy of my certainty... Let's practice: "This world was over a long time ago." The mind that thought it is no more present in that mind than it actually was at the moment that it thought it was separate.

You are in a condition that has no causation. And this is why you grieve. Because when you look for the gratification of your need to be separate, it can not *not* represent the grievance that you maintain in order to sustain the conflict of the limitation that appears to have been imposed on you, but in actuality has no causation whatsoever. So the solution that we are discovering in the Love for each other is nothing but a moment's recognition, somewhere within the matrix of the correspondence of sequential time, that this was the time when the totality of falling in Love occurred, without any need whatsoever that you define it within the complex — the confection of ideas of your attempts to sweeten your sour relationships. [laughter from the camera crew] (I'm going to take that out! No, I'm not going to leave that in. You've got me in confection!)

What happened is, when we come together in correspondences... Say we are the Miracles Healing Center and we are coming together within the matrix of separation, the light-love that we generate together can bring us correspondences — this is called quantum. Or an entanglement that we share somewhere in space/ time can suddenly come joyously into our location and we don't defend ourself. By that I mean this: If all of the power is given to you in heaven and earth and you want to be a vehicle of communication, instead of condemning the concepts of your own mind that are out there, you will simply forgive them and in the process of forgiving is the energy of Love. Listen: There was no possibility you were going to be able to retain and possess the idea of Love anyway.

Since the Universal Mind of the power of everything that is, is an eternal extension, you can not *not* be a part of that. And the idea that you could locate yourself separately is about to disappear in the joy of this encounter.

We began this last half hour with the idea of prayer. Now, the question is not that your prayers are not being answered; the question is, what are you praying for? All you would ever really have to say is: `Father, I will to be as You willed me to be" rather than, "I will to assert myself separate from You." And immediately the power of your creative source would become a part of what you are because it *is* what you are.

One prayer together in that realization and then we will take this encounter within this frame of time and

exercise a major conversion of this continuum of time —
Listen:

For the Father loveth the Son, and sheweth him all things that Himself doeth, and He will shew him greater works than these, that ye may marvel. Listen: *For as the Father raiseth up the dead, and quickeneth them, even so the Son quickeneth whom he will.*

Here is your declaration of release, dear brother: *I am God's Son, complete and healed and whole, shining in the reflection of His Love. In me is His creation sanctified and guaranteed eternal life. In me is Love perfected, fear impossible and joy established without opposite. I am the holy home of God Himself, I am the Heaven where His Love resides, because I am His holy Sinlessness itself, for in my purity abides His Own.*

Let's say it together: *We bring glad tidings to the Son of God, who thought that he suffered. Now he is redeemed And as he sees the gate of Heaven stand open before him, he will enter in and disappear into the Heart of God.*

I am very much aware of, perhaps, your continued rejection of my certainty as I appear momentarily within the dark form. Rejection in the sense that it's very difficult for you, up until now, to see the entirety of the offering. The reason that that is true is because in that particular sense, up until now, you haven't seen it because you were hell-bent on holding that grievance. What you actually learned from me is the idea of grievance or sickness or loneliness or pain or death is a demonstration of death. Remember? Death is an idea that you have about yourself — that is what the grievance is. It is an idea that takes many forms, doesn't it? All of the forms of your conceptual mind, at any single moment, justify the grievance that you hold against your brother, this world, and God.

Now, right now, I showed you, by the action of my mind, what forgiveness is. The simultaneousness of Love, in our communication with each other, was the healing factor that allowed you just for a moment, to disassociate from — what was the first hour? — the arthritis.

In the miracle, it sometimes is difficult for you to see that there is a re-assemblage within the illusion. Look at my hand, here is the hand that you may still believe within your own matrix of correspondence is seventy-six years old. That's crazy. Come on, I don't know what "seventy-six years" is! Apparently, it is your idea that you are on this little planet, going around the sun and you have gone around it seventy-six times — in a Universe that is fourteen thousand million years old? And I am teaching you that you only lasted for a second. And that your nano-second is a billionth of a second, so you are going to be here for a billion years in order to be here for this second.

I am showing you that this is the moment of departure. Not because I say it's so, but because it is the moment of departure because it is the only moment in its entirety, contained within the idea of separation, and the solution has been offered and accepted.

So what I am offering you, from the mind of the resurrection of the bodily association of Jesus, is nothing but the entirety of correspondence with your body association with your brother, in which you merge into a single identity where the grievance against God and your brother disappears.

I promised Him I'd read two more sentences about your condition, and you can decide you don't want it anymore. Remember that the light has come; you can heal and you will heal. And listen to this:

When you shut yourself off from yourself, which remains aware of It's likeness to its Creator, your Self seems to sleep, while the part of your mind that weaves illusion, in its sleep, appears to be awake. Can all this arise from holding grievances? Oh, yes! You bet. *For he who holds grievances denies he was created by Love and his Creator has become fearful to him in his dream of hate. Who can dream of hatred and not fear God?*

One more paragraph, listen: *It is as sure that those who hold grievances will redefine God in their own image, as it is certain that God created them like Himself, and defined them as part of Him. It is as sure that those who hold grievances will suffer guilt, as it is certain that those who forgive will find peace.*

It is as sure that those who hold grievances will forget who they are, as it is certain that those who forgive will remember.

Look at me: You are going to stay a little pissed about my message? Go ahead. If you haven't come far enough along in the idea that I am appearing within your own dream, telling you that as long as you hold a grievance, you never can escape. I hope I got you far enough, so that at least you'll admit that the grievance is against yourself. That is to say, since ideas leave not their source, very fundamentally and most of you conceptually have admitted this, the grievance you are holding against yourself is actually your determination to identify yourself as separate from your creative source. Ok?

I watch you struggle with the retention of your grievances in your *Oprah Show* of nothingness, in your attempts to redefine yourself within the grievance, but never relinquish it. Because if you relinquish the grievance, you would and will discover in your wholeness the Kingdom of God, in which you are a whole part. I don't know if you know what the *Oprah Show* is. I have no idea what that meant! What it actually means is, you come together and share the necessity for the conflict of pain and death and call it Love. It's not Love. It is conflict and death. Stop depending on the necessity of the retention of the grievance, within your own mind, and you will be able to forgive me for my uncompromising message. Who you think I am, in your association with your ego, with yourself, will always deny you access to the entirety of the Love I am offering you, very simply because there is only Love. And the conflict that you feel, in your need to hold on to your own self-identity and suffer the consequences that are self-annihilation, will cause you to believe, within your split mind, that as a part of your mind, I must share your conflict.

I have trained many new associations, in the form of self-recognition, in a moment of forgiveness, that all they really saw reflected back to themselves was a grievance they held against themselves and justified in the guilt of self-identity.

You are whole and perfect as you were created and you have absolutely nothing to say about it. I am an image of correspondences, within your concepts, telling you that it is true and that I have absolutely nothing to say about it. Because we can share a moment of the undoing of our need to identify ourselves as separate.

Jesus — savior of this correspondence and the one to which I have offered the entirety of my allegiance in a dedication, through my own revelation, to offer continuing resurrection — expresses it in a particular way in his *Course In Miracles*. It is going to take about three and a half minutes, maybe four, but I want you to hear it within the idea that it is actually the power of Love that we are sharing together, that goes just past the holy encounter to the idea of the non-defensiveness that will be represented in his resurrection. Will you listen with me?

From *The Journey Back*, Chapter 8 in the *Text*: *If God's will for you is perfect peace and joy, unless you experience only this you must be refusing to acknowledge His Will. His Will does not vacillate, being changeless forever. When you are not at peace it can only be because you do not believe you are in Him. Yet He is in all in all, His peace is complete, and you must be included in it. His laws govern you because they govern everything. You can not exempt yourself from His Laws, although you can disobey them. Yet if you do and only if you do you will feel lonely and helpless, because you are denying yourself everything.*

Why would you want to deny yourself everything, except your fear of the power of mind that I am offering you? No wonder the human world rejects this. It's an idea of the power of separate minds to sustain themselves in the littleness — the incredible littleness of the energy frame of light — that is totally meaningless in the correspondence. This is from Jesus now; this is from a testament of the entirety of this teaching, and I want you to share it with me and read it in your own mind in the first person. Remember when we did *John:17* and Jesus spoke of his Self being yourself. This will be expressed in the first person in this text, but I want you to read it, when you go to read it in the text, as being your declaration. Listen:

I am come as a light into a world that does deny itself everything. It does this simply by disassociating itself from everything. It is therefore an illusion of isolation, maintained by fear of the same loneliness that is its illusion. I said that I am with you always, even unto the end of the world. That is why I am the light of the world. If I am with you in the loneliness of the world, the loneliness is gone. Are you listening from Jesus? *You can not maintain the illusion of loneliness if you are not alone. My purpose, then, is still to overcome the world. I do not attack it, but my light must dispel it, because of what it is. Light does not attack darkness, but it does shine it away. If my light goes with you everywhere, you shine it away with me. The light becomes ours, and you cannot abide in darkness anymore than darkness can abide wherever you go.* Look: *The remembrance of me is the remembrance of yourself, and of Him Who sent me to you.*

You were in darkness until God's Will was done completely by any part of the Sonship. How else could it be perfectly accomplished? My mission was simply to unite the will of the Sonship with the Will of the Father by being aware of the Father's Will myself. This is the awareness that I came to give you, and your problem in accepting it is the problem of this world. Look: *The world must therefore despise and reject me, because the world is the belief that love is impossible. If you will accept the fact that I am with you, you are denying the world and accepting God. My will is His and your decision to hear me is the decision to hear His Voice and abide in His Will. As God sent me to you so will I send you to others. And I will go to them with you, so we can teach them peace and union.*

The most exciting prospect that I could ever experience in my own revelation is your own self-discovery, along with your willingness to accept the mission of this *Course In Miracles*. What we just read together is such a dramatic demonstration of the scripture of Jesus that most of us are at the point where we no longer feel any necessity to simply deny the nature of the requirement that we forgive each other.

I am obviously speaking to you from revelatory mind, in which I find correspondence within the idea of darkness. Now, the light of my mind shines away the darkness — we just read this together — and gives me the totality of the qualification of saviorship, through the power of the mind of God, which we can share together in a moment of correspondence of shining of light, with the realization that each one of us, separately, carries with us from heaven, the light of the Universe. That's why we read together, *You are the light of the world.* The activation of light that's occurring in your body form now will give you a moment of perfection, through His Mind, and now through our minds, that allow me to represent to you, in this time frame, a perfect body.

Power of mind. Will you say this to me? "I am a perfect body." Of course, how would you not be perfect if you're contained entirely in the Will of God? The idea that it's still an illusion can't possibly convert me or concern me, because at any moment I can see the entirety of our correspondence within the fabric of light that previously defined the idea that our bodies were separate.

Look with me, dreamer of the dream: The sole requirement of my offering to you, within your own dream, in this *Advent of a Great Awakening*, is that you recognize responsibility solely within yourself, with no concern about the world. And as you ascend in the entirety of your self-identity, all of those that you previously held within the conflict of your own mind can not *not* enter with you, very simply because they are already in your mind. And when you change your mind they can not *not* change along with you, because God goes with us wherever we go in this renewed excitement of falling in Love together. And in the expression that we can hold it in our hearts, without regard to this world, and thus sustain the moment of the conversion of the separation, in which this world will disappear into the nothingness that it already is.

Will you say it with me as we depart this continuum of pain and death? "God bless us, each and everyone," as we ascend to the Kingdom.

Thank you for the sharing of my uncompromising determination that all of the Source of Reality is contained in our associations with each other. I'll be seeing you very soon.

Love Is A Many Splendored Thing

"Just For You"

Here's a particular reference that I am going to try to teach. They asked me about Love being a many splendored thing, and I looked into my mind and I said, "You mean Love?" This love is a many splendored thing, and the reference I was given from my savior Jesus, whose direction that he asked me to take in a particular reference... May I?

It's a real joy for me to be present with you in this condition. I am going with an idea that I am going to use the word, "Love". With your kind permission I am going to use it in a very particular way, because of the totality of the increased idea about yourself in your dedication that the solution about what we are together as our minds undergo this joyous experience of resurrection. I am privileged, and with your permission as a teacher of God, I am going to use a reference just for a moment. I was out on a high mission outside of this faculty and Jesus is with us, as you know, and in the idea of his presence — he's here now with us — I am going to talk to you just a little bit about Love.

Love, and we came in singing *Love is a many splendored thing...* Let's look real quickly — Jesus is here with us — at the little script that I am going to attempt to perform for about a little cycle of time. I would appreciate very much if you would release (a little) ideas of (perhaps) a withdrawal back into yourself, in regard to what I am feeling about you right now. The reason that is true is my feeling about you right now comes from the whole mind, an enlightened mind, the mind (in our case) of Jesus. So he's going to read to you about a particular way in which you, perhaps, can recognize how very lovely you look to me.

At this moment in our dedication to each other, most of you now had an opportunity to see me as a minister, in my determination, in my return into this space/time reference that we're beginning to meet our brother Jesus all over the place and we had lunch today and I said, "What emphasis should I begin to put now that we're beginning to see a faculties about recognition?" He looked at me and he said in Aramaic, "Rakhma rakhma..." which means it's Love. Teach only Love, because that is what you are, that is what you are, that is what you are, what you are. Will you listen?

I Love You. As the Father hath loved me, so have I loved you: continue ye in my love. Thou shalt love the Lord thy God with all thy heart, and with all of thy soul, and with all of thy strength, and with all thy mind: and thy neighbor as thyself. Come unto me, all ye that labor and are heavy laden, and I will give you rest. Because I am going to give you the rest that I am feeling about you right now, because I love you.

Listen: *I come to you from our Father to offer you everything again. I love all that He created, and all my faith and my belief I offer unto it. My faith in you is as strong as all the love I give to my Father. My trust in you is without limit, and without the fear that you will hear me not,* that you will not hear me. *Love's meaning is your own and shared by God Himself. For what you are is what He is. There is no love but His, and what He is, is everything there is.* Listen: *You are as God created you. Look with me: And so is everything you look upon* regardless of the images that you seem to see. Regardless of the images that you seem to see in correspondence with our need to determine outcomes within our own mind.

The simple truth of the matter is that God is Love, and we're all going to be included in to it, regardless of conditions in which we had previously found ourselves and the possible belief that there could be such a place as other than we are seeing each other at this time, because how we're seeing each other now, there is what Love is. Isn't it? Love is this. This is what Love is.

Let the Love of God shine upon you by your acceptance of me. My reality is yours and His. By joining your mind with mine, you are signifying your awareness that the Will of God is one.

Here we go: *Would you know the Will of God for you?* Here: *Ask it of me who knows it for you and you will find it. I will deny you nothing, as God denies me nothing. Ours is simply the journey back to God Who is our home.*

The joy that I am expressing in feeling in regard to us right now is a simple admission that we're all cognizant of the idea we've been on a very long journey, a very long journey, a very long journey, a journey in which we look for the truth and found some love and then lost it. We found some love and then lost it.

His reappearance here now with us is signifying a new light factor that was previously not a part, and though we had seen it in some of our degrees of intervals of light, it always seemed to get lost again. Didn't it? Didn't it? There it is again. These are the messages from our savior.

These are the ideas that we have always wanted to hear about the inevitability of a perfect moment of recognition of our self together in the whole idea that while we appear to be consciousness identities within this little place of space and time, there was always somewhere within us the idea there must be, there must be, within me, something wherein I may recognize myself in a new place in space/time, because I have been made cognizant of the idea in this message, in this Scripture, that my savior Jesus has given to me that indeed, there is another world, and that that other world can be mine, because the directions I am being given in regard to what Love is have been included in with how we are now catching glimpses of the joy in our relationship with each other.

Oh you are looking very bright, thank you. Thank you again. What's occurring in the advent of the return of Jesus into this cycle of time is very simply an increase in the frequencies of what ostensively are said to be joy and happiness and peace that were actually always a part of what you have been through in your efforts, both to find *and* deny, the access that is actually yours in regard to the absolute inevitability that we are sharing the bright light of a single source of reality which is what we are — what we are, what you are.

Jesus is here, of course, and the readings that are going on are from his mind to yours... to yours... to yours.

The journey to God is merely the reawakening of the knowledge of where you are always, and what you are forever.

I give you the lamp and will go with you. You will not take this journey alone. I will lead you to your true Father, Who hath need of you, as I do. "Who has need of you, as I do." Shall I tell you why? Our Father loves us. And while we appeared to have separated our selves in our idea of our search for peace and happiness, our Lord God is totally indiscriminate in His determination to express the love that He is offering to you and equally determined in your acceptance of it through Jesus, my savior, that the power of decision about what we wanted to see in our own mind in regard to love, was ours to make... was ours to make... was ours to make in the echoing of light that is reaching a new pitch of energy and is going to give many of us a great deal of happiness.

You may be aware of this particular reference in my coming here where Jesus and I were together here just this little time ago, and that he's altering on a continuing basis the frequencies of light by which you are expressing yourself conceptually. The truth of the matter is each time you express yourself, available to you is another you and until you can recognize who that other you is that's actually walking with you on this journey, Jesus will stand here with us... Jesus will stand here with us... with us... with us.

Remember, "I gave you the lamp." And *I will lead you to your true Father, Who hath need of you, as I do. Your Father loves you. All the world of pain is not His Will. Forgive yourself the thought He wanted this for you.* Look: *You cannot understand how much your Father loves you...* You cannot understand how much your Father — the journey that we are now accomplishing — really loves you, *for there is no parallel in your experience of the world to help you understand it.* Listen with me: *There is nothing on earth with which it can compare, and nothing you have ever felt apart from Him resembles it even ever so faintly.* "Resembles it even ever so faintly." My, that was beautiful, not even particularly. So the journey under which we are going to undertake the idea of a new reflection of light, being determined now by our recognition of each other in a particular sense was sort of a condensed idea of a private association within your own mind. Shall we share why? The momentum of the conversion of your mind is inevitably going to come from the seed by which you are recognizing yourself.

For many of us as the energy of love begins to increase in intensity, we find it difficult to verify how we can be feeling so much love and joy when there doesn't seem to be any reason as we peer out into this world and see all of the apparent death and tragedy going on around us — that the other world lives with us at this moment and is offering us continuing conversions of what we want to see in our mind. On this last journey which lasted that cycle of time, we began to meet more and more who have decided to undertake with us the inevitability that the journey that could be accomplished by leaving this association of light and journeying out into the universe was indeed ours to make.

Now, once that determination came into our mind it became unconditional in the idea that there was always something else we could listen to, that the mind and voice of Jesus was offering to us as he spoke directly to us concerning the love that we're feeling about each other. So this little interlude of love was a promise that earlier today we decided to share in coming into this frame.

This little video, this little audio that we're exchanging... For many, many of you now, the whole idea that Jesus is appearing all over this continuum is being expressed in miraculous stories that you're telling about each other, where suddenly those who were suffering incredible pain and loneliness and despondency have suddenly said, "Wait, I heard a voice, I heard something in my mind speaking to me, I have come to listen to an instruction I am being given by a whole spirit of energy that has no concern whatsoever about how I appear to be in this faculty of myself."

So this little interlude of love is more directly concerned about the light energy that I am expressing for you in the recognition that suddenly the neighbors, the brothers, the enemies, those we hated and detested were only ideas we had about ourself within our own mind, and now that love is beginning to come directly from the idea that Jesus is going to be with us.

We looked at it for a moment and he said, "Use a little arbitration," because his practice is always going to be to confront *you*, not someone else. Trust me — my savior Jesus had no idea about alterations of consciousness that allowed you to formulate continuing ideas in space/time. That's not the way the mind thinks. The way your mind thinks is to compare on an eternal basis, continually, ideas of the self concept by which you love other associations and the totality of your own Self in which you love other associations.

Yes, that was a many splendored thing and it's rapidly going on now in the conversion. Here's about Jesus' love, isn't it? Listen: Remember: There is nothing on earth with which it (your love) can be compared, *and nothing you have ever felt apart from Him resembles it ever so faintly.*

God's Will for you is perfect happiness. Only the love of God will protect you in all circumstances. It will lift you out of every trial, and raise you high above all the perceived dangers of this world into a climate of perfect peace and safety.

I ask but this: that you be comforted and live no more in terror and in pain and loneliness and death that's going on in your body form. Do not abandon love.

To your tired eyes I bring a vision of a different world... of a different world... *...so new and clean and fresh you will forget the pain and sorrow that you saw before. This world is full of miracles. They stand in shining silence next to every dream of pain and suffering and sin and guilt. Let us be glad that we can walk the world* just in this little time left, and find so many chances to perceive another situation (idea about our self) where God's gift (Love) *can once again be recognized as ours.* Shall I tell you why that's true?

In you is all of Heaven. Every leaf that falls is given life in you. Every bird that ever sang will sing again in you. And every flower that ever bloomed has saved its sweet perfume and its loveliness for you.

This is from our savior Jesus: *God gives thanks to you His Son for being what you are,* for being what you are. *You are His Own completion and the Source of love along with Him. Your gratitude to Him is one with His to you. For Love can walk no road except the way of gratitude, and thus we go who walk the way to God.* Listen: *You do not walk alone. God's angels hover near and all about.* Him is our love that we share. *His love surrounds you, and of this you can be sure* with Jesus: *that I will never leave you comfortless* or without all the help that you need in this regard. He's right here now isn't he, next to us. Will you have with me that bright conversion that's occurring now in your own mind in regard to this whole idea that God is actually with us and that the voice that we're hearing was actually within our own mind? Perhaps it wasn't necessary that we expressed it? Shall we share why? The communication that is going on between the awakening minds of conceptual self ideas are within our mind, not out in the world.

My discovery of you, right there, in our relationship with Jesus, who is here with us — he just came in, thank you— is an idea that in this faculty of an idea, you just happened to stop by. I was having lunch with my savior Jesus. There are reports coming in about how many of you are leaving a place vacant. One of our oldest traditions in Christianity was to set an extra place at your table. And many of you now are reporting for our satellite in which we're going to reproduce the whole story of the reappearance of Jesus — all of a sudden in a dramatic incident Jesus coming in and sitting down with us. Thank you for inviting me. Do you see that?

When I came into this cycle, I was bringing with me the energy of love that I had felt in my association with Jesus. You listen to me there, conceptual mind. Once that mind of Jesus begins to share with you the certainty of his neighborhood, where you've loved him with your heart and your mind and your soul and suddenly you love your neighbor. You recognize how much joy there is in what's occurring now in this new continuum of time? There is just a moment when we're going to invite another guest of ours to come in,.Is that alright with you?

There's so much conversion goingon out in the world that it's impossible to express it conceptually. But you hold it in your heart, won't you? I'll be right back. Here I am,.I'll be right back with you. I am going to leave you for that moment. God bless us, each one of us. He's coming. Stay right there won't you? I'll be gone that minute and I'll be back.

* * * * * * *

I'm back, I'm back. Now, you were singing together in this interlude on the camera, we were singing together:

I'll be loving you always,
With a love that's true always.
When the things you plan
need a helping hand,
I will understand always.
Days may not be fair always.
That's when I'll be there always.
Not for just an hour,
Nor for just a day,
Not for just a year,
But always.

Thanks for putting up with my efforts to show you the joy I feel in expressing in a script, my determination that I am going to be with you always, with absolutely no regard to how I appear to be in this factoring of my own mind. Shall we say why? We're sharing together individually, in what appears to be our body formulation, that we've been searching outside of our self for an answer to the problem that besets us in the idea that we seem to go through cycles of time within our own mind in which the evidence for which we are searching dissipates somehow and we begin to lose the love that we had and we're told that that's the nature of things.

My savior Jesus, from the time he came into this cycle said, "This is not the nature of things. You are whole and you are perfect as you were created." And that certainty is what "for always" means. That certainty there in that moment of joy was a whole conversion of your mind in what you thought you were.

I am beginning to meet from outside of this framework of time more and more evidence of the raising of the principle of energy that was manifested in the species in the idea of man in his conversion from body form to the resurrection of the nature of who he really is.

Yes, it is about always. It is about always. Listen about "always": *Blessed are they which do hunger and thirst after righteousness: for they shall be filled.*

I will not leave you comfortless: I will come to you. At that day ye shall know that I am in my Father, and ye in me, and I in you. Listen: *Lo, I am with you always, even unto the end of the world.* Here's Jesus now. *When I said, 'I am with you always,"I meant it literally. I am not absent to anyone in any situation* — in any situation. *Because I am always with you, you are the way, the truth and the life.* Look with me: *My mind will always be like yours, because we were created as equals. It was only my decision* that we are now sharing *that gave me all power in Heaven and earth. My only gift to you is to help you make* that same decision with me. Did you see this? *My gift to you is to help you make the same decision* that I have made. Look, see how necessary it is at this point in space/time to continue to decide, very simply because the power of decision in the factoring of my self-concept is one; very literally, where I am deciding the outcomes that I want in regard to where I find myself in this body identity.

In the resurrection of Jesus, the instructions we have accepted in his — let's use Sermon on the Mount for a moment — are simply to recognize that the power of decision was ours to make in regard to what we wanted to see about our self at that moment... at that moment... at that moment. Thank you.

Many of you now are walking around in this idea of a story from the satellite that's been told and the miracles that are beginning to happen in his sudden appearance... in his sudden appearance... in his sudden appearance.

You ready? Shall we teach this for a minute? I am going to teach.

They call me the Old Man. I followed some instructions. I've been through exactly the pain, loneliness and death that our Jesus savior went through, and that you went through, because it's impossible that the decisions that I am making and have made were not correspondences that had trapped me in the idea that I was a body form.

In the re-appearance of Jesus in his resurrection and now in your re-definition of yourself, all you're really saying to me is: I am rising in my mind from the idea of a new bright light that will be present with me in this circumstances of light.

Let me express, in case the opportunity doesn't arise again, because many of you are leaving this cycle of time altogether. I want to say how very grateful I am of the perseverance that once he flashed into your mind as he has with so many of us, when we couldn't find him anymore some of us lost confidence in the idea that he was there. He was always there, but there were moments in us when we became perhaps frightened of the light that suddenly began to ascend or descend onto us in these alternatives, but he is right here and he is right now and he's sharing his togetherness, togetherness with each other — with each other.

Listen: Remember: My only gift to you is to help you make the same decision that we were created equal. *This decision is the choice to share it, because the decision itself is the decision to share. It is made by giving, and is therefore the one choice that resembles true creation.* Listen. Jesus would remind you: *I am your model for decision. By deciding for God I showed you that this* decision can be made, and that you can make it. Look: *My part in the Atonement is not complete until you join it* and give it away. Why? *Of yourself you can do nothing, because of yourself* as a human being *you are nothing.* Look with me: *I am nothing without the Father and you are nothing without me,* because by denying the Father you are actually denying yourself.

A concept of the self is made by you. Look with me from Jesus now directly: *It bears no likeness to you at all. It is an idol, made to take the place of your reality* as a Son of God. *The concept of* yourse*lf, as a human, that now you hold would guarantee your function here,* in space/time, *remain forever unaccomplished and undone.* Listen: *And thus it dooms you to a bitter sense of deep depression and futility. Yet it need not be fixed, unless you choose* (decide in your mind) *to hold it past the hope of change and keep it static and concealed within your* own *mind.*

The secret of salvation is but this: That you are doing this unto yourself. No matter what the form of the attack, this is true. Listen: *Whoever takes the role of enemy and of attacker, this is still the truth. Whatever seems to be the cause of any pain and suffering you feel, this is still true.* It's still only coming from your own mind.

Your goal is to find out who you are, having denied your Identity by attacking creation and its Creator. You're now perhaps ready to listen. *Now you are learning how to remember the truth. For this attack must be replaced by forgiveness, so that thoughts of life may replace thoughts of death* — the thoughts that you've been holding about yourself, as many of us now are witnessing; the destruction of the body, the laying down of the body, the pain, the loneliness, the confrontation that the body holds our self within the idea that I must share with you my body formulation in an identity of who I believe I am.

In this new frequency of light that's being represented by new decisions we have decided to make, we have decided to make another decision. Listen with me. This is the mind now of Jesus. Practice with me, gently: Look again. Look again.. mm... look. In this new aggregation you've discovered by the power of your own mind that you had fixed ideas of your concept on results that you wanted to be true within your own mind, and you inevitably then had to utilize ideas about yourself that you recognize as techniques that you are using in order to verify an accumulation within your self-concept of what you think you are.

The availability of my savior Jesus Christ in a re-identity of yourself in his enlightened mind and now with mine and with yours, is nothing at all within your own concept but an increase in another idea that will be available to you about yourself, if you will release through forgiveness the defensive technique of conceptual mind that you utilize in order to deny you access to that bright light — that bright light that just for the moment relieved you of the necessity to hold on to that conflict of your self -identity within your own mind.

Those of us who are now in this procedure in this worldly endeavor are beginning to spot our selves in recognition of the idea of our mind. Thank you for that. Yes, I see that you just had a glimpse of a light. This is beautiful. The glimpse of the light that we are sharing is not coming from our bodies. Shall we share why? The original light of our body formulation was brought with us when we came into this cycle of time, but it's been dimmed and weakened by the idea that the reflections of space/time light that we've been getting do not hold the entirety of the power of mind — power of mind that you just discovered in our relationship with each other.

Here's Jesus. Look with me, dear one; he's showing up all over the place. Look, he has absolutely no concern about what you are believing about your body formulation. Here, I just stopped by to tell you that. Now, whatever procedure I am using, and this is without regard to how I am garbing myself in a body identity, there is always a new way that I can look at myself, in a new value of love that I am finding in the self confidence of the new certainty of me that is growing in me as it's growing in you.

Your previous uncertainty is changing, isn't it? You're becoming more and more certain about a very private identity you have in relationship with yourself. It's good to meet you again. There's a great deal of joy, and this is going to be just a little interlude in private with us, but I want you to know that this whole idea of telling stories with each other in the miracles that are going on, will be very energetic in the idea of light that you can now hold on to.

Practice with me: Give it away. Good. The best idea you can formulate about your own defensive mechanism is to give it. The amazing thing about some of these stories being told about the video is that there are moments where you've been in deep conflict, you know, where no arbitration was apparently possible and all of a sudden you said, "This is not worth it; here take it." Now, the moment you did that with your mind, the other association perhaps in his new definition of him self said, "Oh, no, wait just a moment, let's look again, let's look again. Let's take another look at where we are in this factoring of our mind. We don't seem to have been able to find peace or joy or happiness in the exchanges we thought were necessary in ideas about our self — now suddenly here's the Savior."

Now, acting as arbitrator individually within your own mind is a successful factor of atonement. Christians, there isn't any secret about this at all. We've already agreed you're doing it to yourself anyway. That was very joyous — thank you. That was very joyous in the idea we're all going to be together in another moment so we're going to practice a whole idea of that conversion of mind, that conversion of light, that conversion — there's an echo —there's an echo of light — there's another one. Look with me: When we came into this particular evidence of our self we began to increase the frequencies of light. It would be inevitable if you're in that body form that you haven't begun to re-examine yourself in the ideas of what you actually want to see out there.

Virtually all that occurs is a moment within your own mind when you said, "There has to be something else. The way I am looking at this right now and I am seeing what's going on in this world is impossible. There has to be another way that I can make application of my need" — listen with me now, important — "to discover a reason for being here." "It seems to me that all the reasons that I have been here in a body form, were to live as best I could within this body frame of reference; to tread my way along a particular path that defined a beginning and an end and be dead.

Here's what's happened with the return of Jesus. He's standing in a new light frame of yours, offering continuing conversion of past and future references — there's a nice one — so that all of a sudden, where we're standing together... May I? May I come to that point? This becomes a circle of Atonement where I begin to recognize you. The simplicity of recognizing you will always be contained in the simplicity of recognizing myself, because I am the cause of you. As Jesus reminds you, this world is being caused by you in your identity of yourself, and when you change your mind, this world is going to change. Jesus can read you one prayer, ok?

The whole basis of the idea once you decide to change your mind is to always offer to God, to the Holy Spirit, the realization that all the decisions you've been making about yourself are not really how God is directing you. The love of God for you is not concerned about your capacity to decide outcomes that you want within your own mind — within your own mind — within your own mind — within your own mind. Listen, listen to this prayer — listen:

Father, I need but look upon all things that seem to hurt me, and with perfect certainty assure myself, 'God wills that I be saved from this,"and merely watch them disappear. I need but keep in mind my Father's Will for me is only happiness, to find that only happiness has come to me. And I need but remember that God's Love surrounds His Son and keeps his sinlessness forever perfect, to be sure that I am saved and safe forever in His Arms. I am the Son He loves. And I am saved because God in His mercy wills it so.

I am he whom God loves, because He has willed it in the mind of the new bright energy that is coming into our individual minds in the recognition that through Jesus' direction we are discovering the love we're feeling for each other. There is a very important factor, isn't there, that we were using in the idea of memory of our conceptual self. We were recognizing the practice, since Jesus returned, that we were actually occupied in an idea in this universe of being here and living within that cycle. We have increased the frequency of the idea of the possibility of self recognition that has allowed us at this moment to suddenly feel that joy — that joy— that idea of love that is within us. Thank you Jesus.

Dear Ones, thank you for that. Many of us now are suddenly feeling bright ideas — listen — for no apparent conceptual reason. Some of us said, "I can't take this anymore." Some of us said, "I need to practice." For some of us — are you listening to me — it occurred for absolutely no reason whatsoever. But you remember this, this script has already been written. The time when you will recognize yourself in your entirety and escape the idea of this conflict has been set. Yet, it's determined by the mind, not by what you're seeing out there. All I am doing with you, with Jesus standing here, is increasing frequencies of decision that it's possible for you to make, in regard to this old body form that you see. And suddenly, right in the middle of a vision of yourself, you are taking on aspects of visions of yourself in symbolization of yourself — you're looking very beautiful to me. All you really need to do is turn to the guy next to you, no matter who he was and say, "Wow, where's all that light coming from?" Where are you suddenly beginning... And he says, "Am I showing that?" And you say, "Yes, how are you doing that conceptually?" And he says, "I am not. I've suddenly discovered that walking with me in this frame of time is this new bright reference in our discovery of the clues we have been given in finding the body form of Jesus." Surprise! He was always walking with us anyway. He was always with us and will be with us and we'll be gone, and will be with us in this conversion of our self. Listen, it'll never be lost again. Once you have that in your mind you're going to carry it with you as you complete this journey.

One more thanks for all the love that you've given me because I love you, and the aspects by which we are viewing each other have allowed me to say to you, "I'll do anything in the universe." And I mean this literally. I'll do anything once I begin to see how inevitable it's going to be that there's another place and time that is available to me in this cycle of time. Because God loves us each and every one and we can say together, "God bless us, everyone." And I'll be seeing you in just a moment as you flashed out of here. You may be getting a call any moment now to take a good solid look at the idea that he's back in this sequence of time. We've had enough ideas of crucifixion; suddenly he's here in resurrection — in resurrection— in resurrection of your mind— in resurrection of your mind.

All About
A Course In Miracles

To many of you now in this accelerated program of awakening, the continuing observation that not a single human being on earth really knows what it is, where it is, where it came from, or where it is going and nothing at all about itself in relationship to the universe that is apparently all around it, is becoming more and more intolerable.

———◆▸◖◗◂◆———

As a transformative imperative, *A Course in Miracles* will perfectly assist and accelerate the necessary confrontation of your objective self-identify and the whole subjective universe that surrounds you, so that you may undergo your inevitable experience of resurrection and enlightenment.

What you are afraid of, and deny through your own possessive fear, is your own illumination; your returning to God-mind or the memory of your transverse from temporal being to the reality of eternal life. So, it is your transition from death to life, from your old meaningless self-existence that is, in reality, long over and gone. It is a teaching of initiation or the determination of an individual mind to come to its own whole Universal Self.

It is the rite of your passage from time to eternity, from the apparent occurrence of separation to the remembrance that you are perfect as God created you. It is accomplished through a bright reassociation of your individual perceptual self-identity. It is an awakening. This unearthly catechism is directing you to the confrontation of the necessity of parting the veil. Every obstacle that peace must flow across is surmounted in the exact same way. The fear that raised it yields to the love beyond, and so the fear is gone.

FOR MORE INFORMATION VISIT: WWW.THEMASTERTEACHER.TV

www.ingramcontent.com/pod-product-compliance
Lightning Source LLC
Chambersburg PA
CBHW060437090426
42733CB00011B/2311

DISCOURSES WITH
THE MASTER TEACHER OF *A Course In Miracles*:
OTHER BOOKS IN PRINT

——————◆ ▸)◀ ◀◆——————

These are anthologies of transcripts of profoundly transformative talks given through the revelatory mind of the Master Teacher of *A Course In Miracles*. They are ideas about the means and method of the recognition of the transformation of our minds and bodies, as we freely escape together far beyond the boundless Universe that is all about us.

Master Teacher's discourses always ignite intensely emotional responses in participants as they begin to undergo their individual mental reassociation and transfiguration. You may have highly charged enthusiastic responses to this wholly dedicated, totally simple, lovingly communicated message of truth. Indeed, this outpouring of freedom-to-create that occurs through the release of your former necessity to retain self-inflicted loneliness, pain, aging and death, is the bright contagion of whole mind.

These talks will act as a catalyst for you, the reader, in your own self identity of space/time, to undergo the experience of enlightenment necessary to fulfill your inevitable purpose for living: to remember you are whole and perfect as God created you.

The following titles are currently in print:

ILLUMINATION • HOW SIMPLE THE SOLUTION • THE PARADOX OF ETERNAL LIFE • TIMELESS VOICE OF RESURRECTED MIND • GETHSEMANE TO GALILEE • INTRODUCING A COURSE IN MIRACLES • THE RETURN OF THE HERETIC • LOVE

——————◆ ▸)◀ ◀◆——————

FOR MORE INFORMATION VISIT: WWW.THEMASTERTEACHER.TV